MOUSIE MAGNET, page 20
FRAMED MAGNETS, page 50

LACY DOILY CONE
page 28

RATTLE DATTLE
page 18

MINI MEMO BOARD
page 49

PEN & PENCIL KEEPER
page 51

NATURE FRAME-UPS
page 32

RICEY MOUSIE, page 24

BRASS PICTURE FRAME
page 38

CONE WREATH
page 30

FOUR-HEART CARD (54)
KEEPSAKE BOOKMARKS (42)
ROCKY BOOKMARK (56)

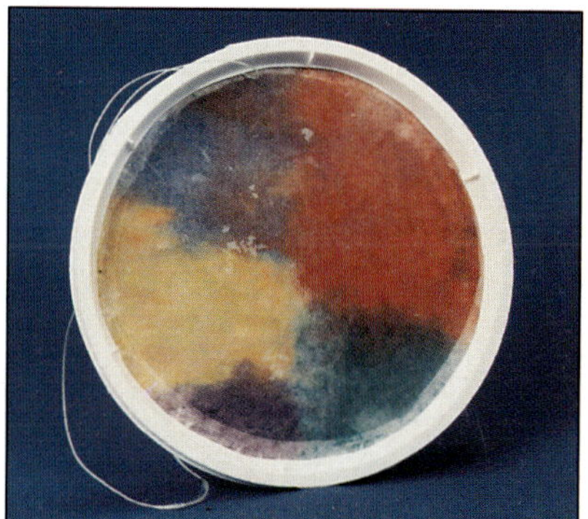

STAINED GLASS SUN CATCHER
page 44

HEY KIDS... LET'S MAKE GIFTS!

Written and illustrated by Leila Peltosaari

This one is for Rina, of course.

Tikka Books, Chambly, Quebec, Canada

Hey Kids... Let's Make Gifts!

Cover photo: Giles Rivest
Other photos: Serge Guérard
Back cover: Elie Albala
Design: Albert Albala

CANADIAN CATALOGUING IN PUBLICATION DATA

Peltosaari, Leila
Hey kids... let's make gifts!: 50 easy ideas to make keepsake treasures

Includes index.
ISBN 1-896106-00-5

1. Handicrafts — Juvenile literature. 2. Gifts — Juvenile literature. I. Title.

TT160.P45 1994 j745.5 C94-900292-5

Please contact the publisher for this book and other titles by the same author.
Published and distributed by:
Tikka Books
P. O. Box 242
Chambly, Quebec, Canada J3L 4B3
Tel. (514) 658-6205, Fax (514) 658-3514

Printed in Canada by Payette & Simms Inc.

ACKNOWLEDGEMENTS

This book is for my daughter, Rina, a source of endless inspiration. Now 13, Rina is at the marvellous age where she connects with the worlds of both kids and grownups. She has always loved crafts and often exclaims, "Give me your craft box! I feel creative today!" In fact, Rina invented several of the designs in this book.

A very special thanks to Michelle Bucheck, Lesley Forrester and Donna Schwerdel for their dedicated copy editing and proofreading. Lesley also "christened" several of the gifts. My appreciation to Marjorie Audet and Renaud Lachapelle who are shown on the front cover.

For terrific ideas, thank you to Dena Bracken (for Brass Picture Frame), Pirkko Kauhanen (for Snowflake Angel) and Ulla Lehtonen (for Love Row Tree Ornament). Thank you also to Barbara Bell, Ellen Dick, Sébastien Guérard, Margaretha Hefti, Ainsley Lewin, Maarit Peltosaari, Anita and Saila Reiniö, Aune Viertola, and Karen and Lorne Walls, for their encouragement and help.

For their contagious enthusiasm and delightful comments, many thanks to the children in the Daycare Centre of William Latter School of Chambly, Quebec: Tiffany Atkins, Karine Boisjoly-Létourneau, Gabriel Comeau, Vanessa Comeau, Shawn Grisanti, Stephanie Lindsay, Steven Lindsay, Christopher MacKenzie, Michael MacKenzie, Samantha Messenger, Emilee Newin, Robert Niedzielski, Carl Olivieri, Michael Tessier, and Christine Samborsky, their Supervisor, Cathy Gatien, and Attendant, Brenda Whitteron.

CONTENTS

CHRISTMAS GIFTS

Dear Kids,

When I was a little girl, I lived on a small farm in Finland with my parents, three sisters, a Samoyed dog, a cat without a tail, and a great selection of farm animals. We had lots of spare time — especially in the winter — when the hay was in the barn, the potatoes and beets were in the cellar, and the wild berries had been made into jam. We had no TV in those days, so we skied and built snow castles, enjoyed reading and knitting, invented stories and plays, and made Christmas tree ornaments and gifts with our friends.

Craft supplies were limited, so we improvised. Borrowing the stiff shears that Mom used to trim the sheep, we cut paper, rough metal wire and delicate cellophane. We rescued the cardboard from sugar boxes, sneaked the prettiest bits of fabric from Mom's sewing pile and begged for leftover yarn to wind into colorful cords. True luxury treasures were store-bought crepe paper, cellophane and foil papers.

Today's kids are as eager to work with craft supplies and to make gifts as we were back in the good old Fifties. Anybody can *buy* a mass-produced gift (with a bit of money, that is) but a handmade gift is always special and unique. There is pleasure in the making and more pleasure in the giving. Kids love to give, but on a limited allowance, it is hard. You might need a dozen gifts! Put your money into nice craft supplies instead and you can make lots of little keepsake treasures for pennies.

I will show you dozens of simple ideas to make lovely gifts for anyone and any occasion. Because many gifts have a practical aspect (such as a refrigerator magnet, Christmas ornament, bookmark, lacy potpourri, etc.), you will be happy to see your gifts in use. I hope that this book will give you and your friends many happy hours of gift-making.

Love,

Leila

P.S. A note to grownups: The use of this book goes beyond the home. Teachers, Scout and Guide leaders and craft instructors constantly need new ideas for children to make crafts and gifts. These ideas are easy enough for children to make, but you don't have to be a child to enjoy this book.

GETTING STARTED

Work space

Creative work can get a bit messy at times. Check with a grownup to find a place where you have enough space to spread out your materials as needed. Protect the table with vinyl or old newspapers. Wear old clothes.

Work with clean hands so that you will have neat results. Read the instructions carefully before you start to know what supplies are needed and how much time and work are required. When you trace the patterns, save them in a big envelope so they're ready if you need them again.

When working with glue, use a toothpick if you need just a dab; use a brush for larger projects. Sometimes it's practical to pour a bit of glue on waxed paper so that you do not soak the brush in the glue bottle.

When you have finished, clean your tools and work space. Keep your craft supplies organized in a box or drawer. Use transparent plastic bags to separate your felt scraps, pipe cleaners, wooden beads and other materials. Then you'll always know what you have.

Safety first

Almost all of these gifts can be made with simple and safe supplies and tools like nontoxic, water-soluble glues and scissors with rounded tips. Ask an adult to help you with those few gifts where you need a hot iron, sharp-tipped scissors to cut rigid plastic containers or lids, a sharp needle to sew, or a nail to push a hole into a cardboard tube.

Tiny jingle bells, wooden beads, strings and yarn look tempting for toddlers and pets to play with, but they might swallow them. If you have toddlers or pets in your home, be absolutely sure to keep all your craft supplies out of their reach.

Supplies

Ordinary household items, trash and nature provide most of your craft supplies. The rest you will find in stores and mail order catalogs.

These items are common in most households or can be bought in local stores:

❑ Aluminum foil
❑ Brush (for glue and decoupage paste)
❑ Cardboard
❑ Construction paper
❑ Cords and strings
❑ Cotton balls
❑ Crayons
❑ Darning needle
❑ Dental floss
❑ Dry beans
❑ Glue stick
❑ Iron (with adult's help)
❑ Knife (blunt, to cut styrofoam)
❑ Lace scraps
❑ Markers
❑ Masking tape
❑ Mason jar lids (rims only)
❑ Nail (to puncture holes)
❑ Paper towels or toilet paper
❑ Pen and pencil
❑ Photos
❑ Plastic bags (transparent)
❑ Plastic wrap
❑ Potato peeler or pencil sharpener
❑ Rice
❑ Rubber band
❑ Ruler
❑ Scissors
❑ Self-adhesive tape
❑ Toothpicks
❑ Typing paper
❑ Waxed paper
❑ White liquid glue
❑ Yarn

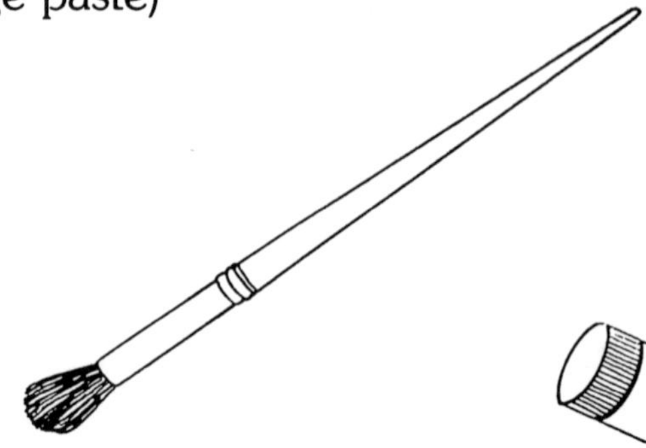

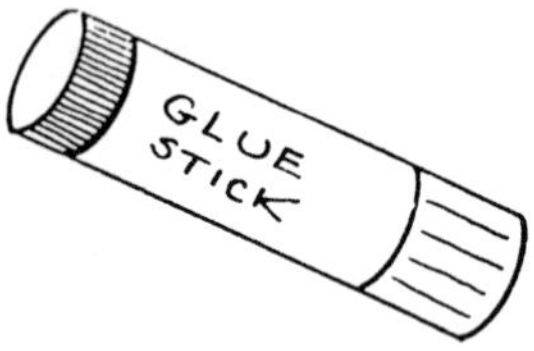

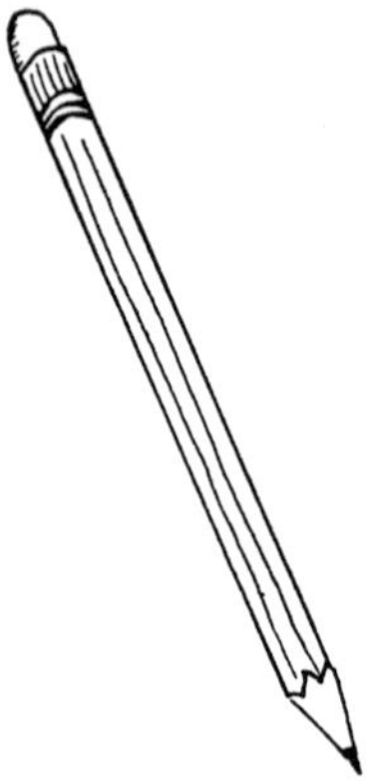

Rescue these items from the trash:

- ❑ Bleach bottles
- ❑ Comic pages from the weekend paper
- ❑ Bottle caps (from small cosmetic and food bottles)
- ❑ Corks (natural, straight corks from wine bottles)
- ❑ Dairy containers and lids (from yogurt, cottage cheese, ice cream etc.)
- ❑ Foil inner seals from dairy and peanut butter containers
- ❑ Gift paper (used)
- ❑ Glass jars
- ❑ Jar lids
- ❑ Magazines, catalogs (to cut pictures from, and to use those white pieces of heavy paper opposite ads or perfume samples — they are perfect for bookmarks!)
- ❑ Milk cartons
- ❑ Old pantyhose
- ❑ Plastic caps from large spray cans
- ❑ Plastic or cardboard containers, large and sturdy
- ❑ Ribbon scraps
- ❑ Soft drink cans
- ❑ Soup cans
- ❑ Styrofoam trays
- ❑ Telephone directory pages
- ❑ Toilet paper tubes
- ❑ Travel brochures
- ❑ Tuna cans
- ❑ Used stamps

Mother Nature yields these treasures:

- ❑ Blossoms and flower petals to make potpourri
- ❑ Cones (from pine, spruce, cedar, tamarack, alder)
- ❑ Flower petals, leaves, blades of grass to dry
- ❑ Flowers with stems to dry for doily cone
- ❑ Pebbles
- ❑ Sand
- ❑ Seashells to fill a gift jar

Stores and mail order catalogs sell these supplies:

❑ Acetate sheet protector (from stationery store)
❑ Allspice (whole berries), in bulk from food store
❑ Balloons

❑ Big buttons (from sewing supply store)
❑ Carpenter's glue for wood
❑ Chenille stems (also known as pipe cleaners), 12" (30 cm) long, and tinsel stems (metallic pipe cleaners)
❑ Corks (natural corks for wine bottles)*
❑ Crepe paper
❑ Curling ribbons
❑ Decoupage paste, matte and glossy (Podgy, Podge, Mod Podge)**
❑ Doilies
❑ Double-sided tape
❑ Felt squares (from sewing supply store)
❑ Gift paper
❑ Glitter
❑ Jingle bells and liberty bells

❑ Lace
❑ Onionskin paper (from stationery store)
❑ Pompoms
❑ Poster board (also known as Bristol board)

❑ Potpourri
❑ Pushpins
❑ Raffia (from florist or mail order catalogs)
❑ Ribbons
❑ Roll of self-adhesive magnetic strip
❑ Self-adhesive silver metallic paper
❑ Self-adhesive transparent vinyl
❑ Stickers
❑ Styrofoam balls (from florist or mail order catalogs)
❑ Tacky glue***
❑ Tissue paper
❑ Tracing paper (waxed or tissue paper is a good substitute)

❑ Wooden beads

* **Corks (from wine bottles):** You can rescue an occasional cork from a wine bottle. If you need lots of corks for a group, you can find them in stores or mail order catalogs for winemaking supplies at just pennies each. For the designs in this book, I have used natural, straight corks, which are approximately 1 1/2" x 7/8" (4 cm x 2 cm).

** **Decoupage paste (also known under the following trade names: Podgy, Podge, or Mod Podge):** This is one of the most versatile and practical craft materials around. It is used for several ideas in this book. A glue, glaze and sealer all in one, in matte or glossy, you can brush it on any surface. It is nontoxic and cleans up with water. You will find it in craft stores and mail order catalogs. Get a large jar! You will be using it again and again. (If you do not have decoupage paste, dilute ordinary white liquid glue with water and use it as a substitute.)

*** **"Tacky" glue:** This nontoxic, water-soluble craft glue is amazingly practical for virtually any project when regular white glue won't do. Tacky glue is thick, white and strong, yet flexible. It is clear when it dries and it doesn't soak in. It is perfect for felt, pine cones, styrofoam, fabric, gluing wooden beads on cork tops, and many other projects. Craft stores and mail order catalogs carry it. Get a large jar so you won't get caught without it!

If you do not have a craft supply store near you, there are several mail order catalogs that carry thousands of arts and craft supplies, including group packs and craft kits for children. A few are listed here:

Canada

Crysbi Crafts Inc.
RR 3
High River, Alberta T1V 1N3
Send $4 for 76-page catalog. (Color insert.)

Lewiscraft
40 Commander Boulevard
Scarborough, Ontario M1S 3S2
Send $2 for 82-page annual color catalog. (Canada only.) Arts and crafts supplies. Mail order and 77 retail stores in Canada.

United States

Craft Catalog
6095 McNaughten Centre
Columbus, OH 43232
Send US$2 for a 112-page catalog.

Craft King
P.O. Box 90637
Lakeland, FL 33804
Send US$2 for a 104-page catalog.
Tel. (813) 686-9600, Fax (813) 688-5072
Order line only: 1-800-769-9494

Crysbi Crafts Inc.
185 Main St.
Umah, AZ 85364
Send US$2 for 76-page catalog. (Color insert.)

Dick Blick
P.O. Box 1267
Galesburg, IL 61402-1267
Tel. (309) 343-6181, Fax (309) 343-5785
Send US$4 for a 500-page color catalog.
Mail order and 38 stores nationwide.

Enterprise Art
P.O. Box 2918
Largo, FL 34649
Order line: 1-800-366-2218, Fax (813) 536-3509
Send US$1 for a 92-page color catalog.

Factory Direct Craft Supply
P.O. Box 16
440 Conover Dr.
Franklin, OH 45005
Tel. (513) 743-5955
Send US$2 for a 62-page catalog.

Kirchen Brothers
Box 1016
Skokie, IL 60076
Tel. (708) 647-8997, Fax (708) 647-8997
Toll-free fax order line: 1-800-323-4715
Send US$2 for a 48-page catalog (color and b/w).

Vanguard Crafts
P.O. Box 340170
Brooklyn, NY 11234
Tel. (718) 377-5188, Fax (718) 692-0056
Free 68-page color catalog. (Minimum order $25.)

POINTY PICTURE FRAME

Cut and fold cardboard squares to make lovely frames. Decorate the frame with markers or gift paper to make each one different. Change the square size to make smaller and larger frames.

You will need:

- ❑ Two 5" (13 cm) squares of thin white poster board
- ❑ Small piece of thin white poster board (or piece of cord) for hanger
- ❑ Ruler, pencil, scissors, glue stick
- ❑ Crayons, markers, or gift paper to decorate the frame
- ❑ Self-adhesive tape
- ❑ 4" (10 cm) square of acetate (from sheet protector)
- ❑ Masking tape
- ❑ Photo, cut into 4" (10 cm) square

What to do:

1. On one poster board square, place the ruler from corner to corner. Draw a line starting and ending 1 1/4" (3.3 cm) from each corner. Draw a second line through opposite corners, again 1 1/4" (3.3 cm) from each corner. Cut these lines open. (Fold the square first into a triangle so it is easy to cut.)

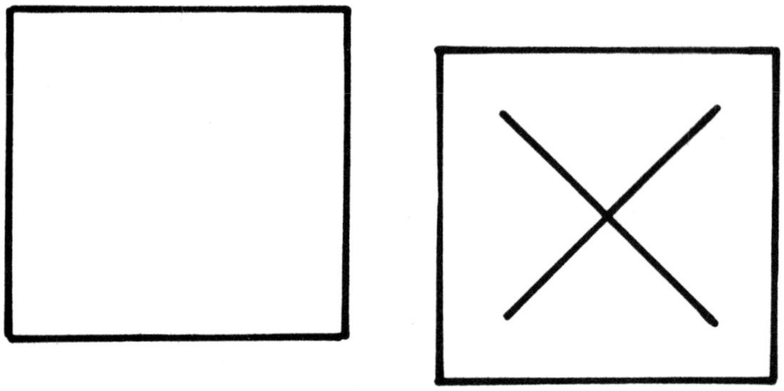

2. Fold each of the four flaps up and then backward, away from the center. Press the folded triangles tightly flat and glue them in place with a glue stick. Place a heavy book on top until the frame is dry.

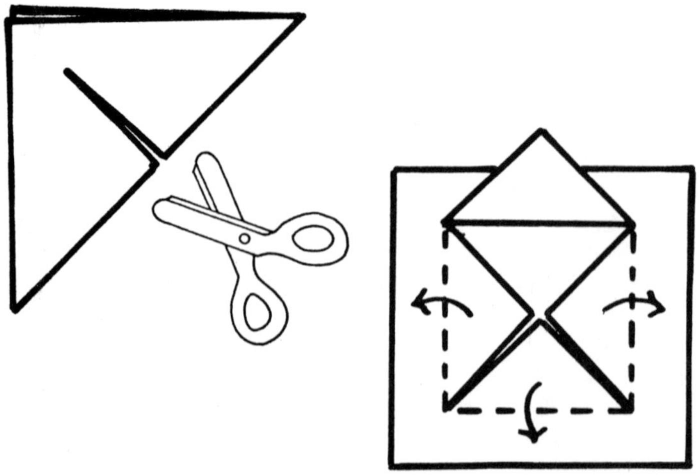

3. Color and decorate the front side of the frame with crayons. (Instead of crayon decorations, glue gift paper on the front and back of the top square before cutting the lines open. Use a different color or design of gift paper on front and back.)

4. Tape the acetate square to the back of the frame.

5. Run a glue stick along three edges at the back, leaving the fourth edge free. Press the second poster board square tightly to the back.

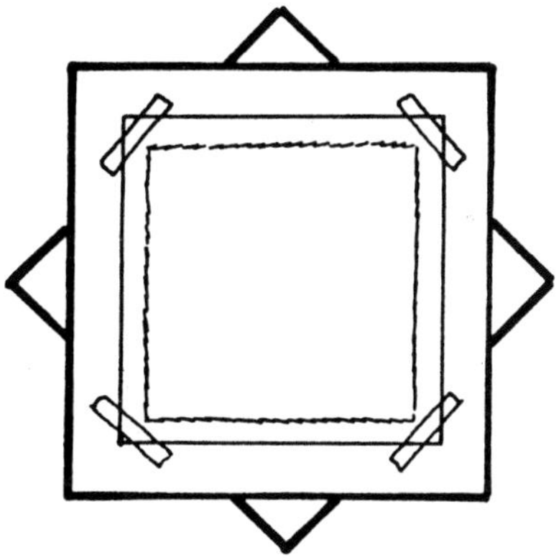

6. Cut a piece of poster board as shown to make a hanger (or use a piece of folded cord) and attach it at the back with masking tape. (The open edge of frame is at the top.)

7. Slip the photo into the frame.

GIFT BASKET

Use an ordinary small bleach bottle to make this beautiful basket. (Wash the bottle very well.) Fill the basket with something nice like bath oil beads, pretty seashells, cotton balls, potpourri, candy...

You will need:

- ❑ Straight, round plastic bottle (small bleach bottle is the perfect size), 4" (10 cm) wide
- ❑ Scissors
- ❑ Double-sided tape
- ❑ Sheet of gift paper to cover the basket and sheet of tissue paper for the lining
- ❑ Wide masking tape
- ❑ One yard (90 cm) of ribbon

What to do:

1. Cut off the lower part of the bottle for the basket. It should be about 3" (8 cm) high. From the leftover top, cut a 1" (2.5 cm) wide strip to make the handle (see illustration).

2. Cut a square from the gift paper and the tissue paper, each about 14" (36 cm) wide. If you use a larger bottle, make the paper squares bigger.

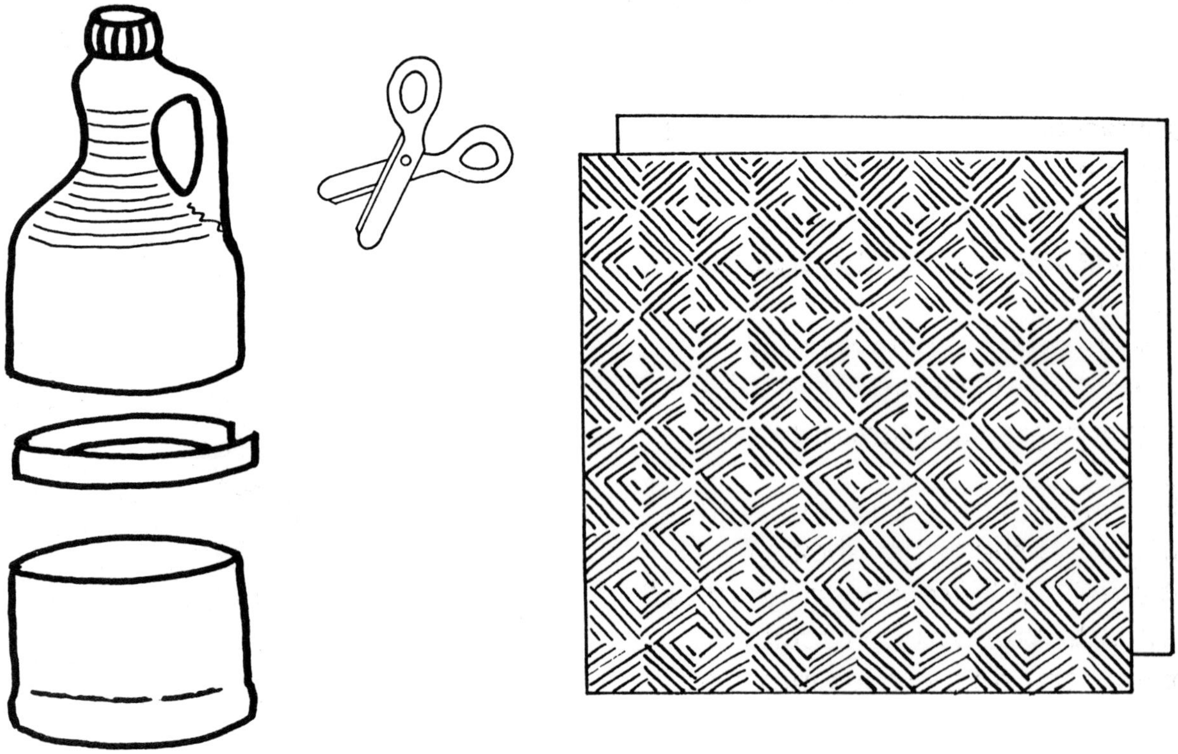

3. To line the basket, stick a piece of double-sided tape on the inside center bottom of the basket. Line the basket with the tissue paper square, centering the paper, and attaching it to the tape. Use more tape around the inside bottom edges and the inside top edges to hold the paper in place. Let the paper edges extend above the top of the basket.

4. Cover the handle. Cut long strips from the leftover tissue paper and wrap them tightly around the handle, using double-sided tape to attach it at each end. Attach the handle ends securely to the outside of the basket with long pieces of wide masking tape.

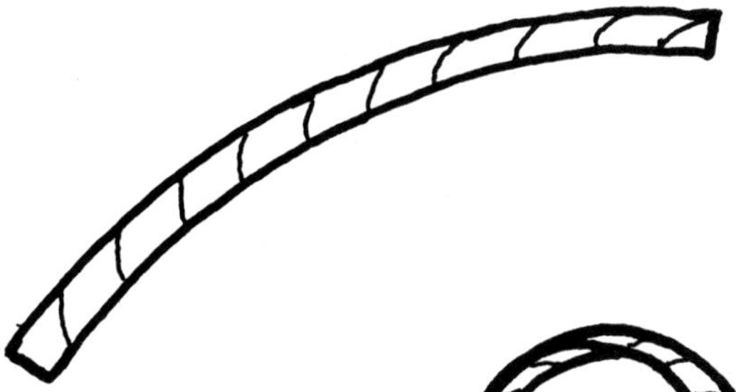

5. To cover the basket, place the gift paper square on the table, colored side down. Stick a piece of double-sided tape in the center of the paper and place the basket on it. Stick more tape around the outside top edge of the basket, then gather the gift paper up (covering the handle ends) and press it onto the tape. Let the paper edges stick straight up.

6. Trim the top edges of both gift and tissue paper sheets to about 1" (2.5 cm) above the rim all around. Wrap ribbon around the basket and tie the ends into a bow.

LACY POTPOURRI

This potpourri frame looks pretty in the bathroom or closet. Who would guess that it's made from a plastic lid and pantyhose!

You will need:

- ❑ Medium-sized dairy container with lid (from cottage cheese, yogurt or sour cream), about 4" (10 cm) wide
- ❑ Scissors
- ❑ 12" (30 cm) of string
- ❑ Glue stick
- ❑ Silver or white doily, 7" (18 cm) wide
- ❑ Potpourri, about 1/4 cup (50 ml)
- ❑ 6" (15 cm) square from an old pantyhose leg
- ❑ Masking tape

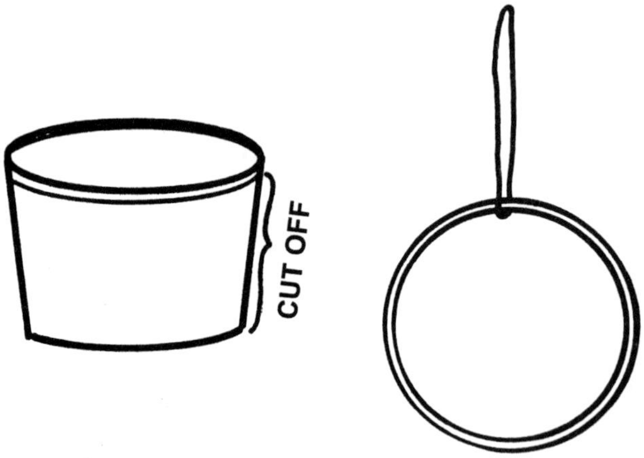

What to do:

1. Cut off the lower part of the container, keeping only the rim.

2. Tie the string around the rim to make a loop for hanging.

3. Place the lid upside down on the table and rub the lid top with the glue stick. Center the doily on the lid, right side up.

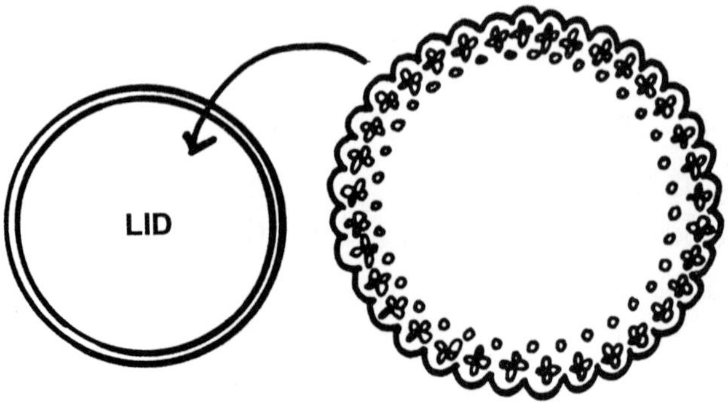

4. Put the potpourri in the center of the doily. Cover it with a square of pantyhose leg. Stretch each of the four corners out and stick them to the tabletop with pieces of masking tape.

5. Press the rim from the lower part of the dairy container upside down on top of the lid and snap them together.

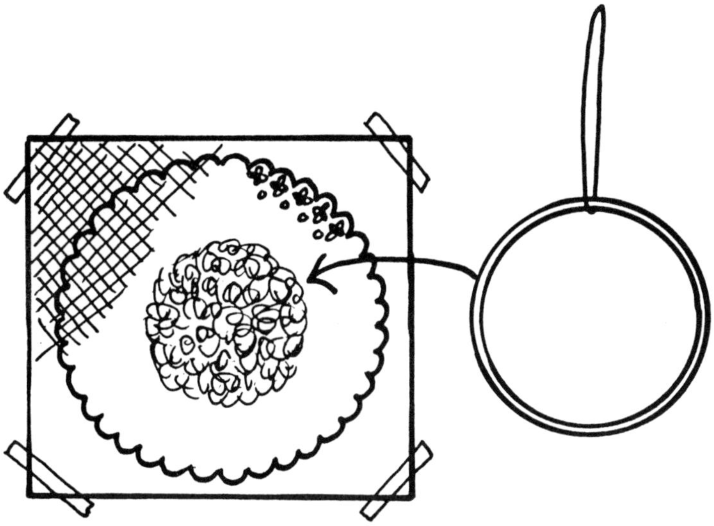

6. Remove the masking tape. Trim off the excess pantyhose from around the outside of frame. Be careful not to cut the string or the doily.

How to make potpourri: You can buy a big bag of potpourri in bulk for a few dollars but it's not difficult to make your own mix. Collect pretty, fragrant flower blossoms or petals, spread them out on a plate (or in a brown paper bag) and let dry very well in a warm, dark place. Mix the dried petals with a sprinkle of salt and brown sugar (to absorb the moisture and to help preserve them). You can add a tiny bit of herbs and spices and perhaps some perfume if you like. Experiment and discover! Store the potpourri in a covered jar. Dried flowers smell great all by themselves but you are not limited to flowers alone; cedarwood chips, pine or balsam fir needles, citrus fruit peels, flower leaves, etc. all give interesting and delightful aromas to a potpourri.

RATTLE DATTLE

Just tape two discarded lids together, filled with beans, and decorate all over with felt. This paperweight rattles!

You will need:

- ❑ Two identical deep jar lids (e.g. from instant coffee)
- ❑ Beans, rice or small pebbles
- ❑ Wide masking tape
- ❑ Felt scraps in assorted colors
- ❑ Crayon
- ❑ Scissors
- ❑ Tacky glue

What to do:

1. Fill one lid with beans, rice or small pebbles. Put the second lid on top of the other one, upside down. Wrap wide masking tape around the edge to seal the two lids together.

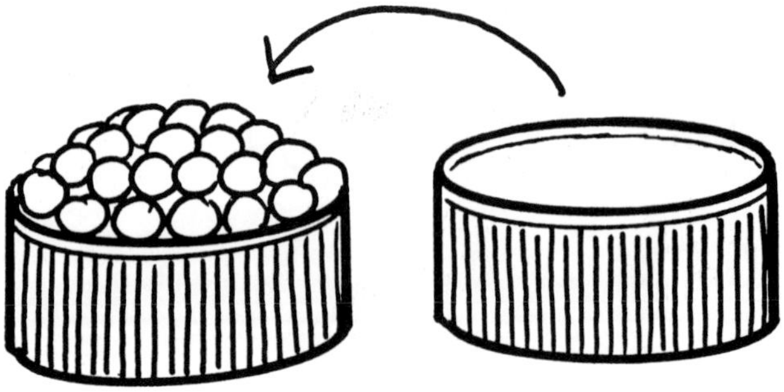

2. Measure and cut a piece of felt to fit all around the side, from top to bottom, and glue it in place. (Make a pattern first from a piece of paper.) Trim the edges neatly.

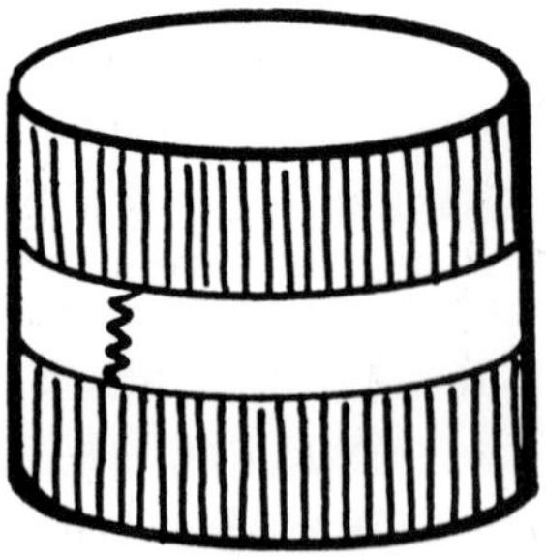

3. Measure and cut felt circles to cover the top and bottom of the lids and glue them in place. (Using the crayon, make a pattern by tracing around the lid circle on a piece of paper or directly onto the felt.) Trim the edges neatly.

4. Glue felt cutouts on the top and around the edges to decorate and individualize the paperweight. A few examples are shown below.

MOUSIE MAGNET

Make this cute mouse from tiny felt scraps. It holds notes on the fridge door.

You will need:

- ❑ Tracing paper and pen
- ❑ Scissors
- ❑ Scraps of gray, black and white felt
- ❑ Stiff cardboard (or plastic lid)
- ❑ Tacky glue
- ❑ Black chenille stem, 5" (13 cm) piece
- ❑ Dental floss
- ❑ Piece of self-adhesive magnetic strip

What to do:

1. Cut two circles from the gray felt and one circle from the stiff cardboard, 2" (5 cm) wide each. (Or use a plastic lid instead of cardboard.)

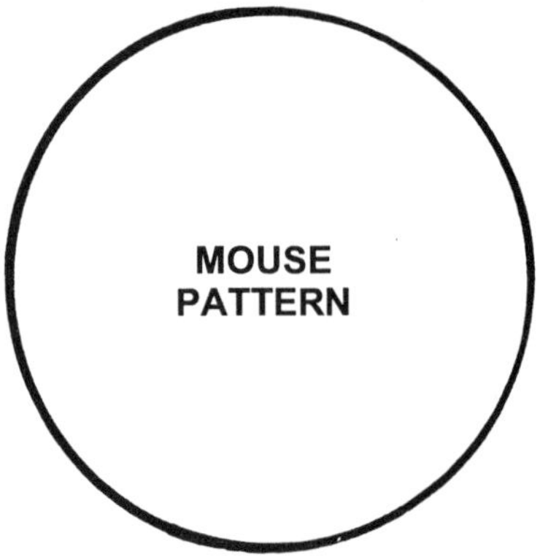

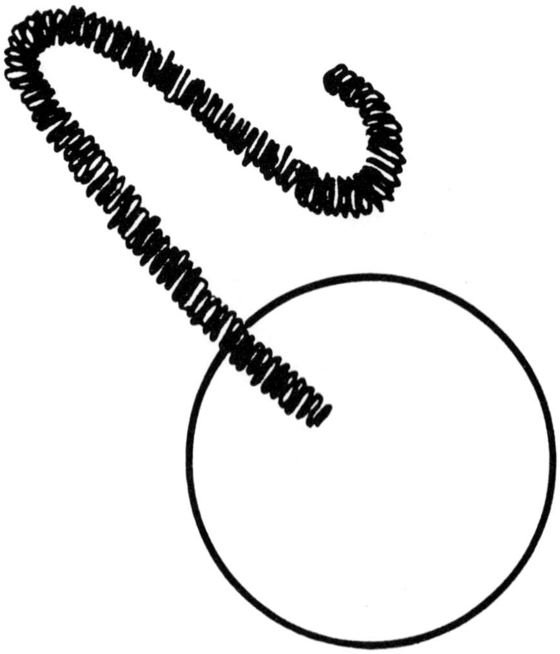

2. Glue one end of the chenille stem onto one gray felt circle to make the tail. Then glue the cardboard circle on top. Then glue the other gray felt circle on top of the cardboard circle.

3. To make the whiskers, take four pieces of dental floss, 4" (10 cm) long, and knot them together in the middle.

4. Cut a small triangle from the black felt for the nose. Put a dab of tacky glue under the center knot of whiskers and stick the whiskers on the face. Glue the nose on top of the knot.

5. To make the eyes, glue white circles on the face. Then add smaller black circles on top of the white ones. (You can also buy rolly eyes in a craft store.)

6. Cut two round ears from the black felt. Put a dab of tacky glue under the back edge of each ear and glue the ears in place, pointing forward. Pinch the back edges slightly so that the ears stick upward.

7. Glue the magnetic strip on the back.

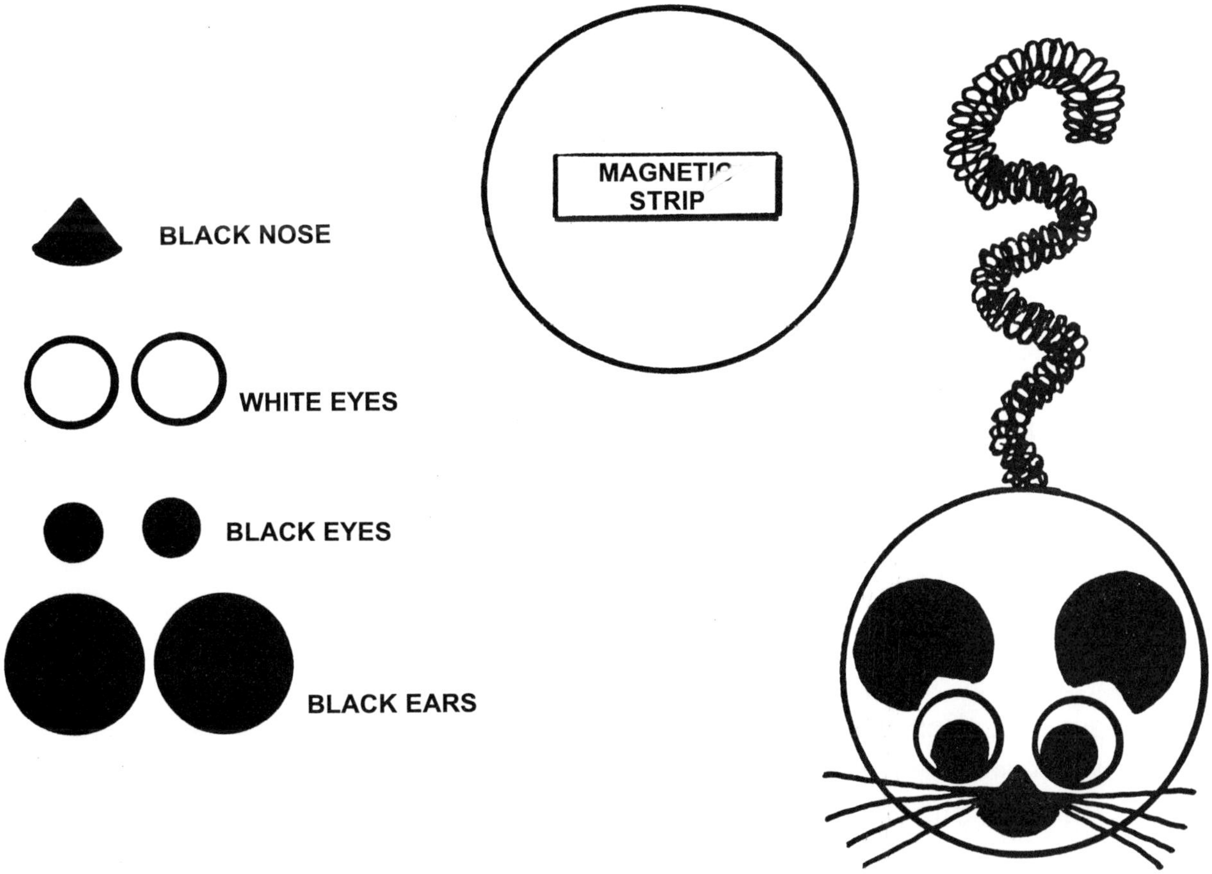

NAPKIN CADDY

Rescue a humble milk carton from the trash and dress it up as a beautiful container. Choose the colors of gift paper and ribbon to match the decor or holiday colors (such as Christmas or Easter). Buy a package of pretty table napkins to fill the box. Make similar boxes, perhaps using a larger carton, for note paper and pens.

You will need:

- ❑ Milk carton, one quart (litre) size
- ❑ Ruler, marker, scissors
- ❑ Tissue paper (two colors or designs, one for lining, one for outside)
- ❑ Decoupage paste and brush
- ❑ One yard (90 cm) of fancy braided ribbon
- ❑ Tacky glue

What to do:

1. Rinse the milk carton. Mark the cutting line with a ruler and marker and cut the carton, as shown. (Discard the top part.) Wash the lower part and dry it well.

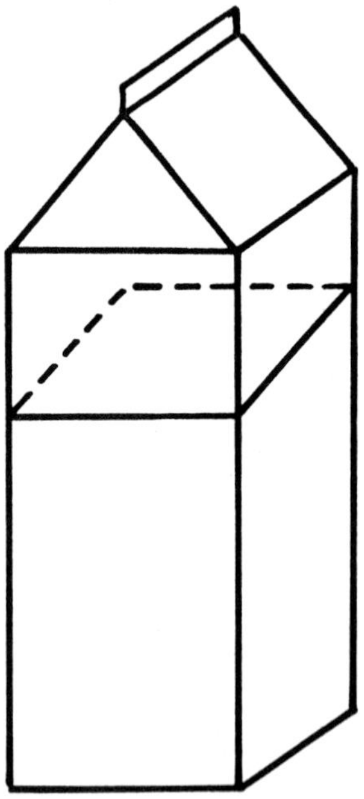

2. Line the box first. Tear off small pieces of tissue paper. Brush decoupage paste on the inside of the box, a small section at a time, and paste the paper pieces on it, slightly overlapping. Brush more paste on top.

3. Cover the outside of the box with the second tissue paper. Again, tear off small pieces and brush and paste them, edges overlapping, covering all sides. Use decoupage paste both underneath and on top of the paper. Let dry well. (If you cut the pieces of solid colored tissue paper, instead of tearing them, you will get a lovely "stained glass" look.)

4. Using tacky glue, glue decorative ribbon all around the top and bottom edges, joining the cut ribbon ends neatly at the back in the middle.

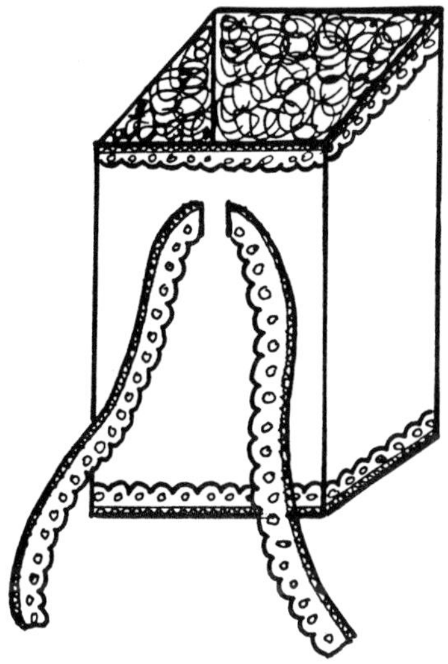

5. Cut two small slits on the center front as shown. Slip a 10" (25 cm) piece of ribbon into one slit and back through the other one. Then tie the ribbon ends on front into a nice bow.

RICEY MOUSIE

This funny felt fellow is filled with rice so he can sit on a table, window sill or bookshelf. This mouse requires a little bit of sewing to close the edges, but it is very easy.

You will need:

- ❑ Tracing paper and pen
- ❑ Scissors
- ❑ Gray felt
- ❑ Black and white felt scraps
- ❑ Two black chenille stems
- ❑ Tacky glue
- ❑ Darning needle and gray yarn
- ❑ Three tablespoons of uncooked rice

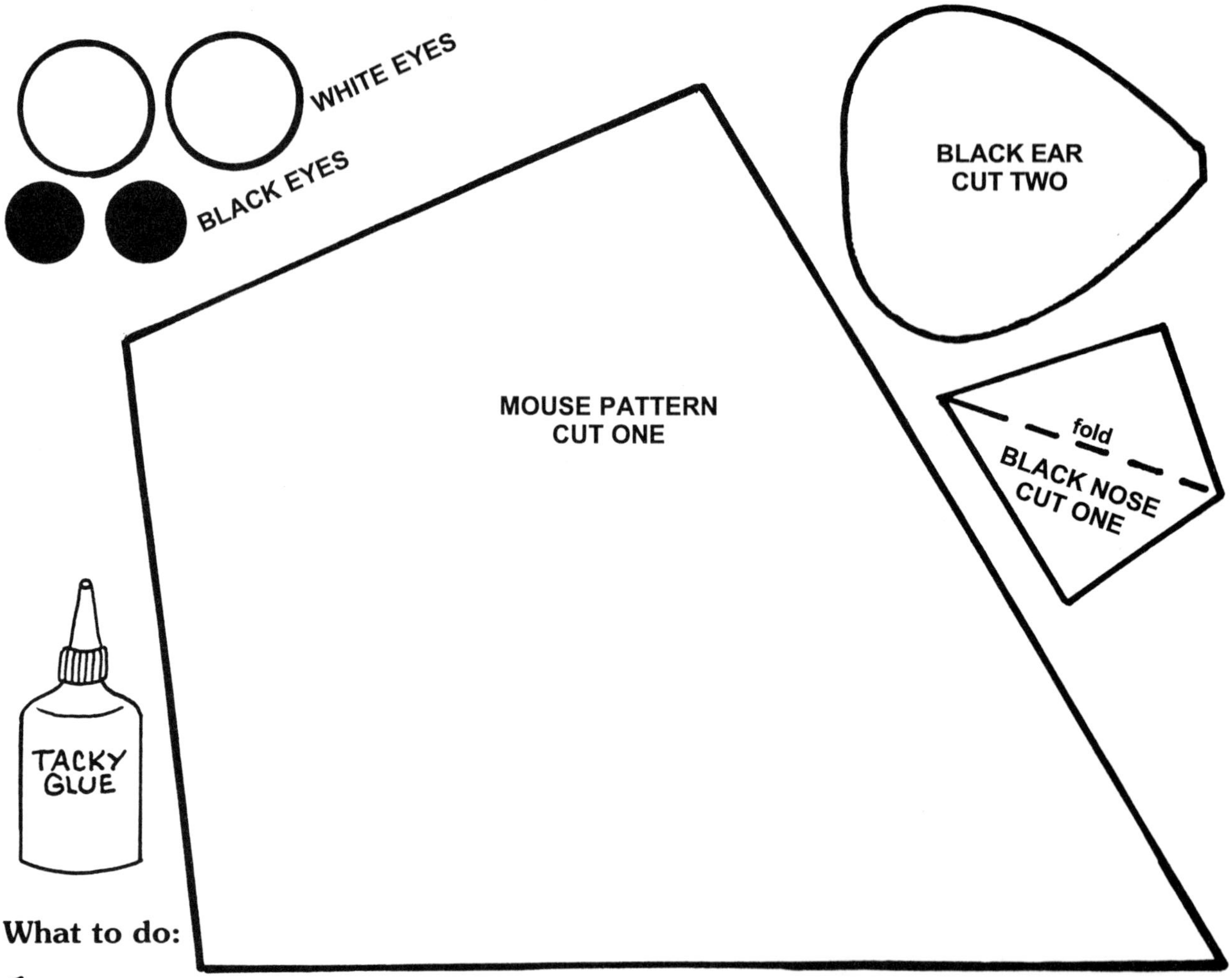

What to do:

1. Trace the patterns onto tracing paper and cut them out. Cut the mouse from the gray felt. Cut ears, nose, and smaller eye circles from the black felt. Cut larger eye circles from the white felt.

2. Using the tacky glue, glue the chenille stem to the inside of the gray mouse body, along the center bottom (to shape and stabilize the bottom), from edge to edge, letting the end extend as a tail, as shown. Still on the inside, use a dab of tacky glue and glue the ear bottoms along the top edge of the gray felt, as shown.

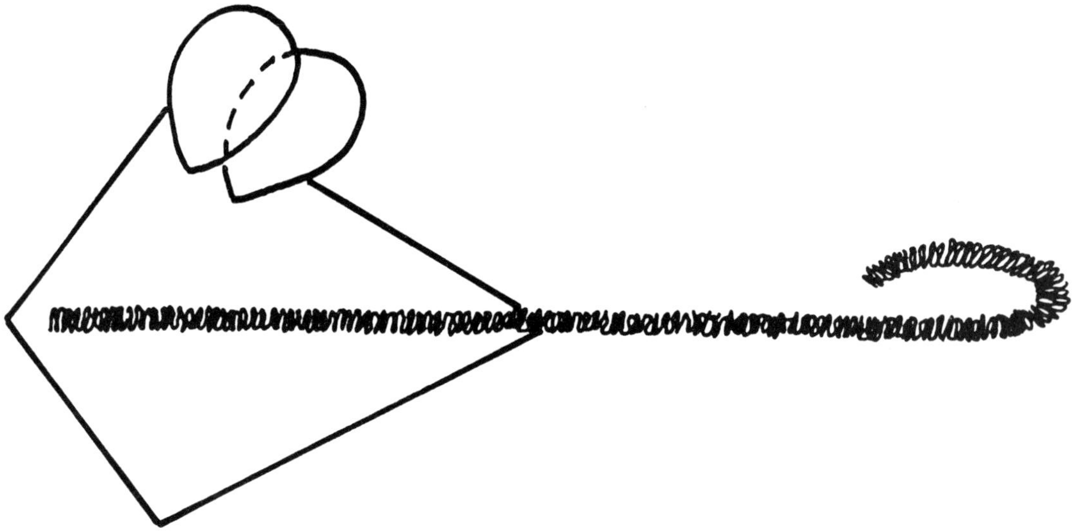

3. Fold the felt in half, right side out, with the chenille stem and ear bottoms inside and the tail sticking out the back.

4. Cut the other black chenille stem in half and twist the two pieces together in the middle for the whiskers. Using overhand stitch (see the box on page 26), start sewing the front edge from nose to the top of the head. Sew the whiskers, where shown (run the yarn through the center twist of the whiskers). Use small stitches.

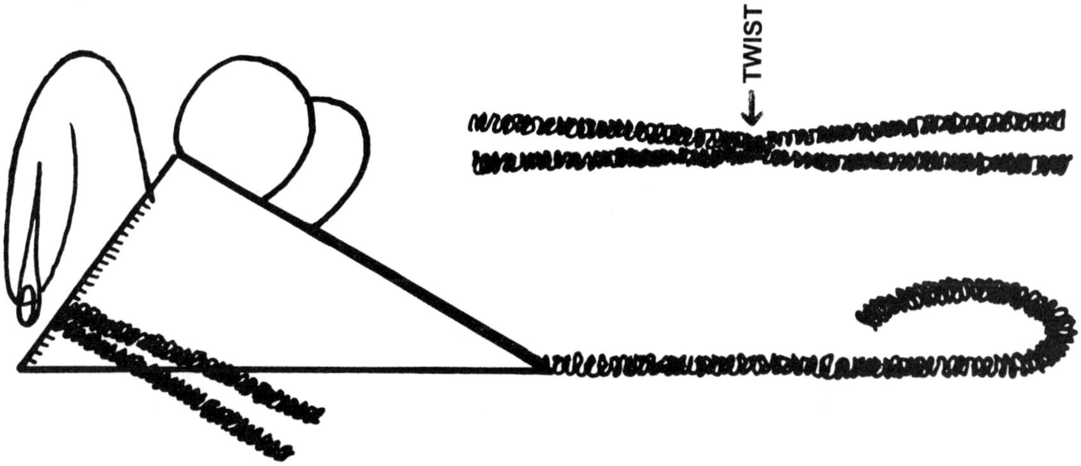

5. Sew the top of the head (through ears) to the middle of the back. Push three tablespoons of rice through the opening into the mouse. Sew the remaining part from the middle of the back to the tail.

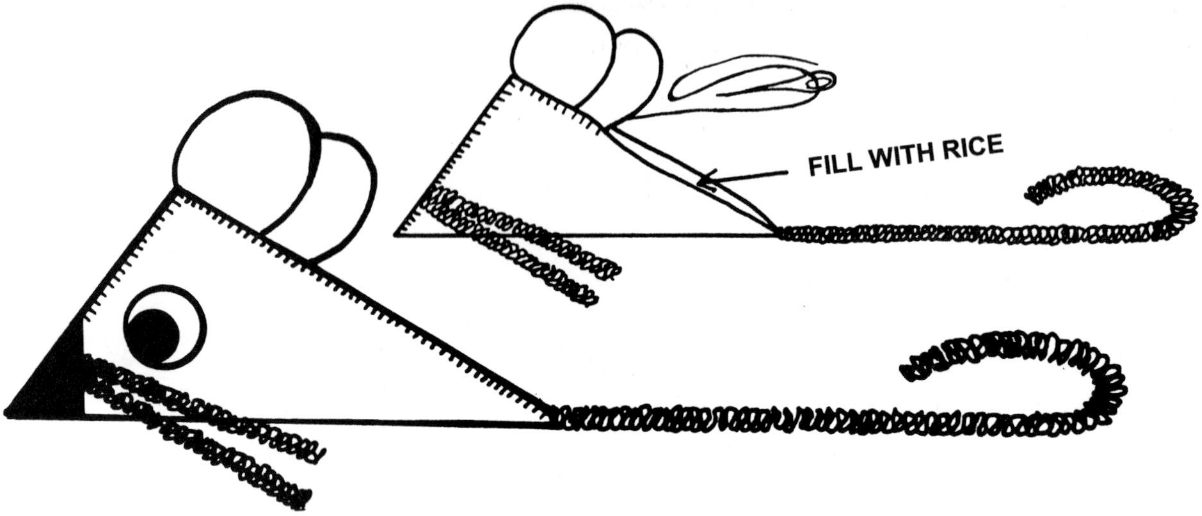

6. Using tacky glue, glue on the eyes, white circles first. Then glue on the smaller black circles, as shown. Glue the felt nose in place with the folded center on top of the whiskers and the cut edges along the bottom edge.

How to sew overhand stitch: Cut a piece of yarn about the length of your arm. Push one end through the needle's eye and knot the other end. Starting between the two felt layers so that the knot is hidden, push the needle to the front edge. Pull until all the yarn comes through. Bring the needle over the top edge to the back, then push it from back to front edge through both felt layers, near the previous stitch, and so on. Make small, even stitches. Do not pull the yarn too tightly. To finish off, sew two stitches over the top of the last one. Then push the needle a bit backward between the felt layers, along the edge, and cut the yarn.

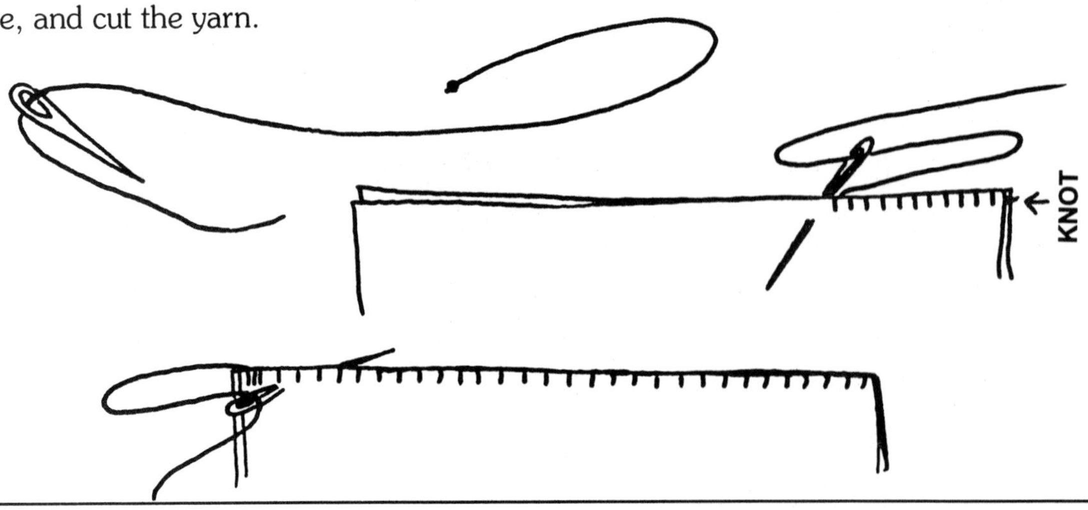

BOOK BOX

A sturdy plastic oil or vinegar container becomes a neat desktop bookcase. This is a practical gift for kids and teenagers. Mom can use it to store her countertop cookbooks.

You will need:

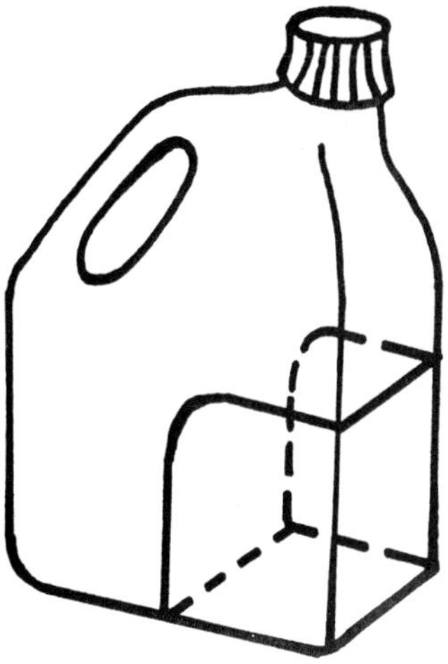

- ❑ Large sturdy plastic or cardboard container with square or rectangular bottom
- ❑ Wax crayon or permanent marker
- ❑ Scissors
- ❑ Small pictures from catalogs, magazine cutouts or tissue paper
- ❑ Brush and decoupage paste (or white liquid glue, diluted with water)
- ❑ Glue stick
- ❑ Felt

What to do:

1. Containers from cooking oil, vinegar, spring water, laundry detergent, etc. are perfect. Using the illustration as a guide, mark the cutting lines on your container. It should be about 5" high and 5" wide (13 cm x 13 cm). Ask a grownup to do the cutting, rounding off both top corners. Wash the corner section well.

2. Cut small pictures of book covers from a book club catalog, use magazine pictures, or tear off small pieces of tissue paper. Brush decoupage paste on the outside of the container (but not on the bottom), a small section at a time, and paste the paper pieces all over, overlapping the edges. Continue until the surface is covered. Brush more paste on top. Let dry thoroughly.

3. Cut a piece of felt, rub the glue stick on the bottom of the book box and glue on the felt.

LACY DOILY CONE

For Mother's Day or Valentine's Day, this charmingly simple doily cone is a lovely gift. Fill it with dried flowers or silk flowers, potpourri or bath oil beads.

You will need:

- ❑ Round doily, 7" (18 cm)
- ❑ Transparent self-adhesive vinyl, cut into two 8" (20 cm) squares
- ❑ Scissors
- ❑ Chenille stem
- ❑ Self-adhesive tape
- ❑ Double-sided tape
- ❑ Curling ribbon
- ❑ Dried flowers with stems (or paper or silk flowers)

What to do:

1. Remove the backing and press the self-adhesive vinyl squares on both sides of the doily. (If you like, write a greeting like "Happy Mother's Day" or "Happy Valentine's Day" on the doily before putting on the vinyl.)

2. Trim excess vinyl from around the doily but leave a narrow border to keep the edges sealed together.

3. Fold the chenille stem in half to make a loop. Tape the lower ends to the wrong side of the doily, as shown.

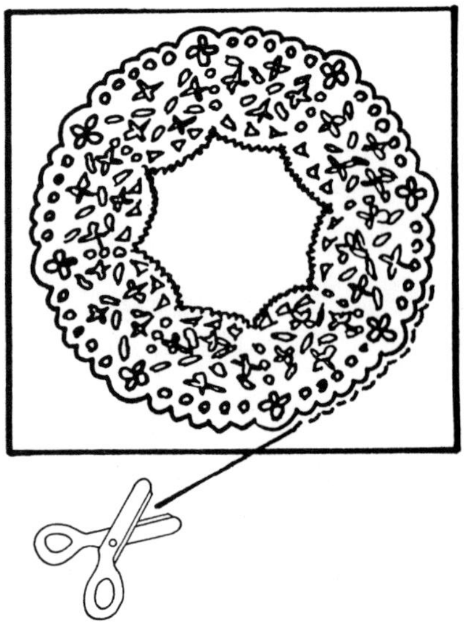

4. Roll the doily into a cone. The chenille stem will be on the inside at the back edge. Bring the side edges to the front and overlap them. Stick pieces of double-sided tape between the overlapped edges and seal them closed.

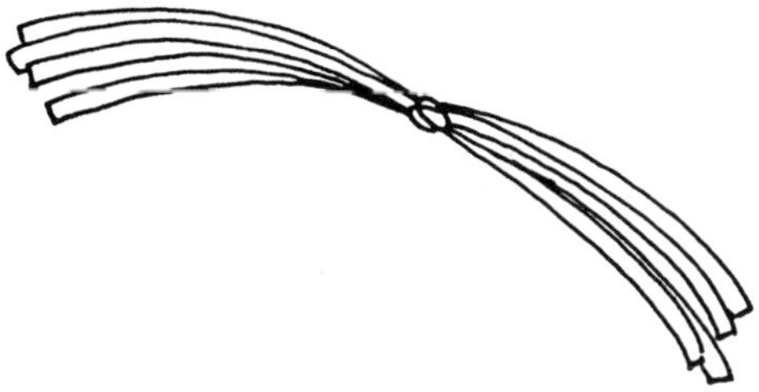

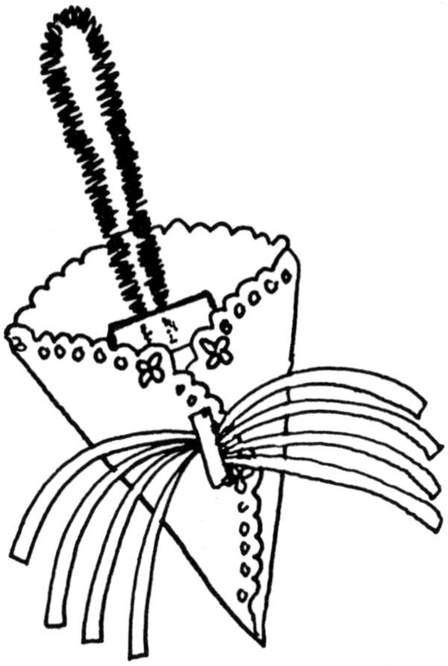

5. Knot several pieces of ribbon together in the middle. Curl the ribbon ends with the blade of the scissors. Tape the curled ribbons to the center front of the doily cone.

6. Fill the cone with dried flowers or silk flowers. The chenille stem loop makes a handy hanger.

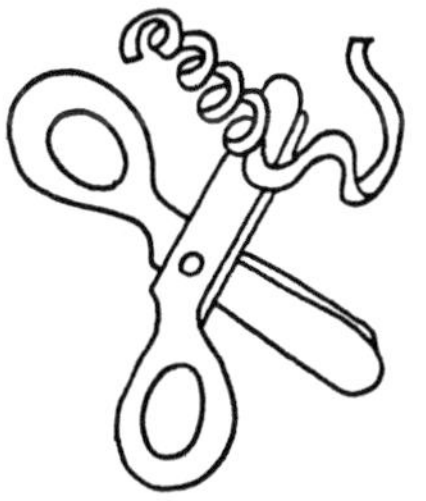

How to dry a bouquet of flowers:

Cut flowers with long stems. Tie the stems together and hang them upside down in a dark, dry place. They will be stiff and ready in about two weeks.

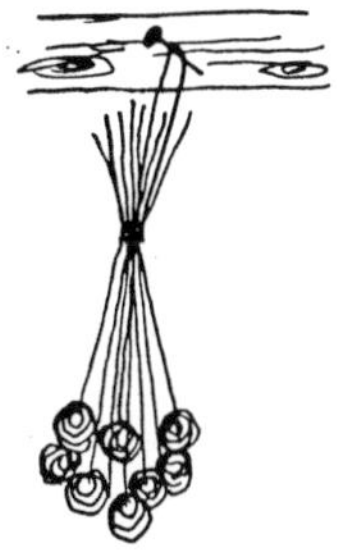

CONE WREATH

This is a gift from Mother Nature. Find small cones under trees and glue them into a lovely wreath. (Spruce cones would be best for this wreath since they are narrow and oval-shaped.)

You will need:

- ❑ Tracing paper and pen
- ❑ Scissors
- ❑ Stiff cardboard (or plastic lid)
- ❑ Black or white crayon
- ❑ Brown felt
- ❑ Tacky glue
- ❑ Small cones
- ❑ Cord
- ❑ Ribbon

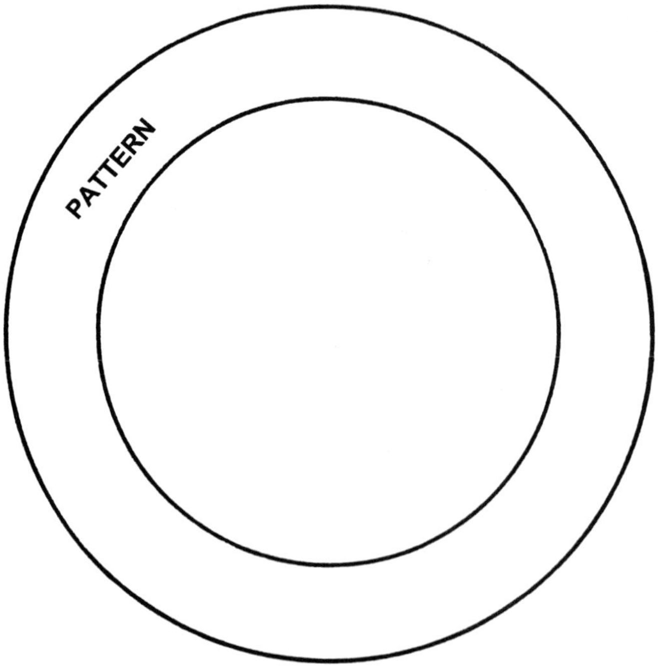

What to do:

1. Trace the ring pattern onto tracing paper and cut it out. Trace the pattern onto cardboard and cut it out. (If your cardboard is not very stiff, cut two rings and glue them together to make the ring stronger. Or use the plastic lid from a medium-sized dairy container instead of cardboard.)

2. Using the crayon, trace the cardboard ring twice on the brown felt and cut the rings out. Using the tacky glue, glue the two felt rings on both sides of the cardboard ring.

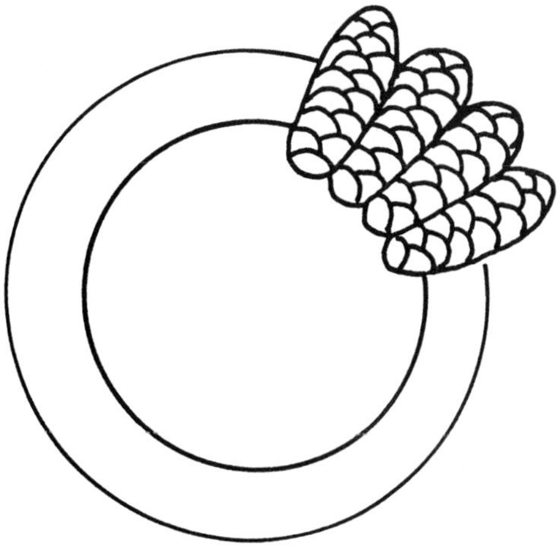

3. Spread tacky glue generously on the felt top of the ring. Press the cones into the glue, side by side, all around, as shown. Let dry very well.

4. Tie a loop from the cord for hanging.

5. Tie the ribbon into a bow at the top of the wreath.

NATURE FRAME-UP

Dairy containers with lids make marvellous snap-together frames. Use the frames as unique sun catchers to display beautiful dried flowers and leaves.

You will need:

- ❑ Medium-sized dairy container with lid (from ice cream, sour cream, cottage cheese, etc.)
- ❑ Scissors
- ❑ 12" (30 cm) of string
- ❑ Thin, transparent plastic wrap
- ❑ Decoupage paste and brush
- ❑ Dry leaves, flower petals, grass blades, etc.

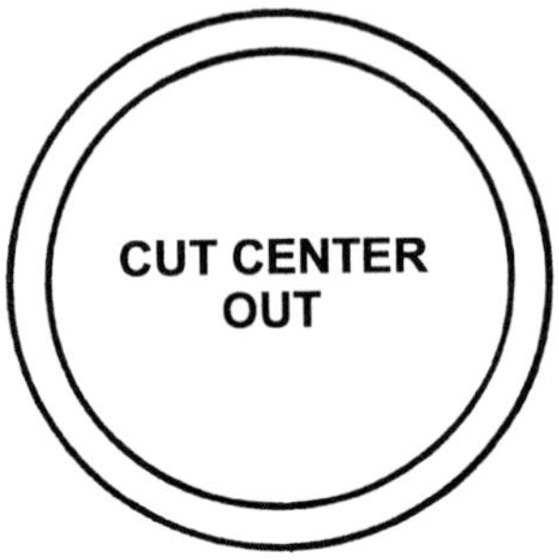

What to do:

1. Make a frame from the dairy container by cutting out the lid's center, keeping only the rim. Then cut off the lower part of the container, keeping only the rim.

2. Tie the string around the lid rim to make a loop for hanging.

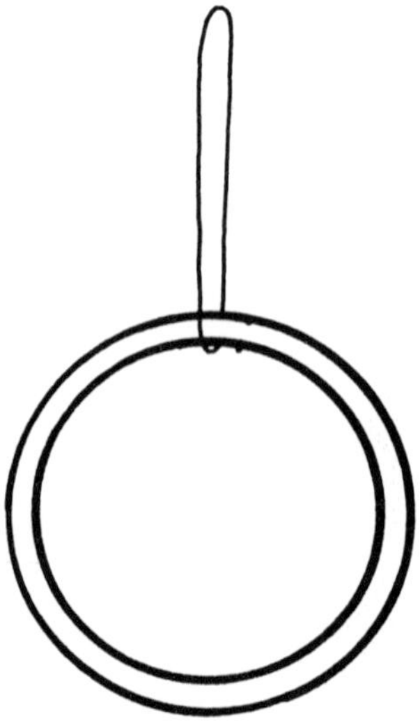

3. Put the lid rim upside down on the tabletop, place a sheet of plastic wrap on top, then snap the container rim in place so that the plastic is straight and tight between the two rims. Trim off the excess plastic all around the outside of the frame. Be careful not to cut the string!

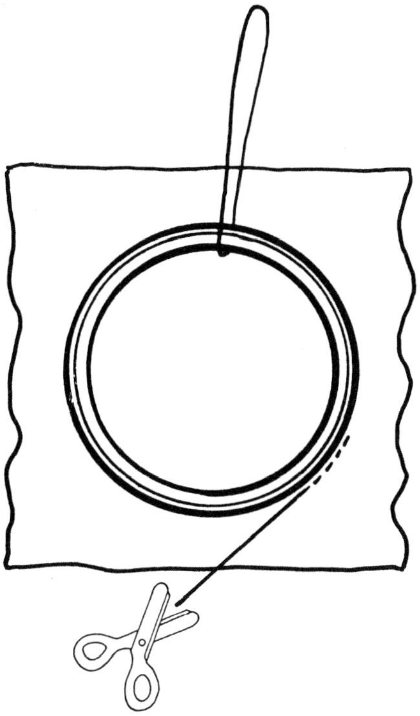

4. Place the frame on the tabletop right side up (the "right side" is the lid rim since it is prettier). Brush decoupage paste all over the plastic wrap which is stretched tight inside the frame. Arrange the dry leaves or flower petals nicely on it, right side up, and very gently brush more paste on top. Let dry so the petal or leaf colors will become vivid and clear. (The top will dry in minutes. It will take a day or two for the paste to become transparent between the leaves and the plastic.)

How to dry leaves and petals: Place leaves or flower petals, etc. inside the pages of a telephone directory, arranging them flat and side-by-side, not overlapping. Allow them to dry for a week or more. Some flowers and leaves lose their color if you dry them too long; if that happens, you can delicately paint them with watercolors.

CORK CUTIES

These are such fun to make and dress up that you will want to create a whole bunch of them! Each cutie will be different, depending on clothes and hair color. (See examples on inside front cover.)

You will need:

- ❑ Corks (from wine bottles), one for each cutie
- ❑ Scissors
- ❑ Wooden beads, natural color, 1" (2.5 cm), one for each cutie
- ❑ Tacky glue
- ❑ Curling ribbon in different colors for hair
- ❑ Scraps of tissue paper, crepe paper, felt, velour paper, chenille stems, thin floral wire, fabric scraps, etc. in assorted colors, to make clothing and accessories
- ❑ Black fine point permanent marker

What to do:

1. Hollow out the cork top about 1/4" (6 mm) deep with the tip of the scissors, as shown with the broken line in the illustration.

ARMS (one piece, about 3" or 8 cm long)

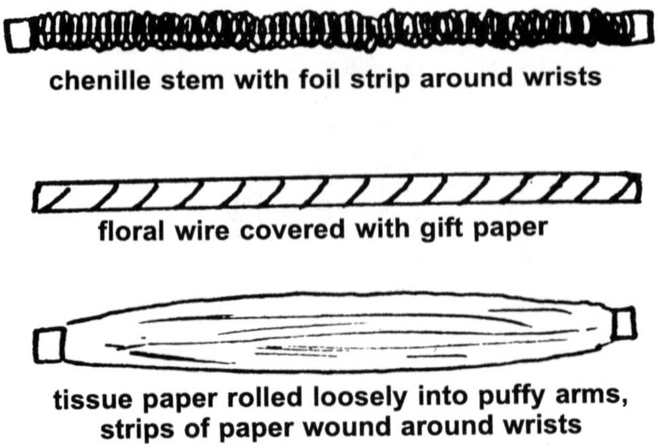

2. Make one long arm by rolling a strip of tissue paper, or cover floral wire with gift paper, or use a piece of chenille stem.

3. Dress up the cork body by making clothes from tissue or crepe paper scraps, gluing them on with tacky glue.

4. Glue the center of the long arm into the carved hole of the cork top with arms extending to each side.

5. Using the tacky glue, glue the bead head on cork top. Hold the head tightly in place for several seconds so that the glue will hold.

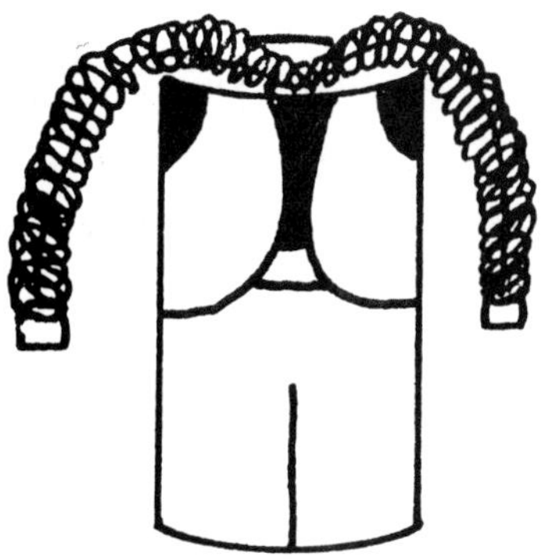

6. Cut a piece of curling ribbon and curl it by pulling it against the blade of the scissors. After you have curled it, split the ribbon into several very narrow strands to make "hair". Glue the curly hair on top of the wooden bead. If desired, make accessories such as a hat (cover bottle cap with felt), bow or scarf from crepe paper or fabric scraps.

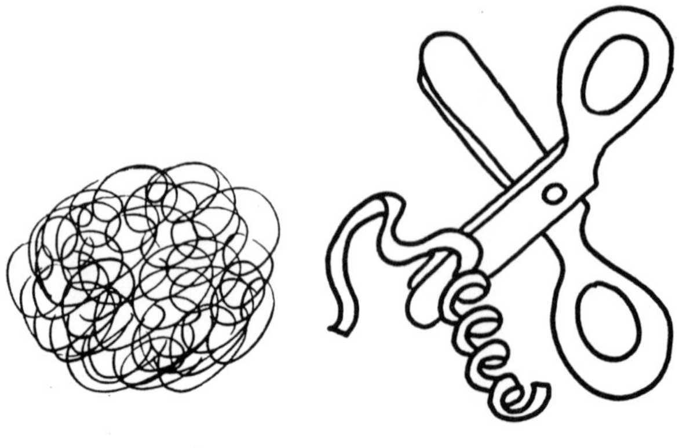

7. Draw eyes.

WIGGLY WILL

This silly little worm wiggles at the touch of your finger. Amuse your friends with this gift!

You will need:

- ❑ Red chenille stem
- ❑ Pencil
- ❑ 1" (2.5 cm) white pompom
- ❑ Tacky glue
- ❑ Black and green felt scraps
- ❑ Scissors
- ❑ Tiny bottle cap
- ❑ 2" (5 cm) wide jar lid

What to do:

1. Wind the red chenille stem around the pencil into a tight spiral. Remove the pencil.

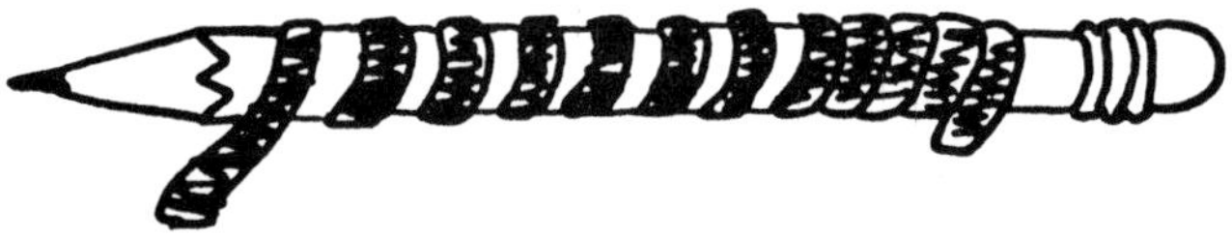

2. Glue the white pompom head on top of the spiral.

3. Cut tiny squares from black felt and glue them on for eyes. (Or buy rolly eyes from the craft store.) Make a hat by covering a tiny bottle cap with black felt, add a small brim, and glue the hat on.

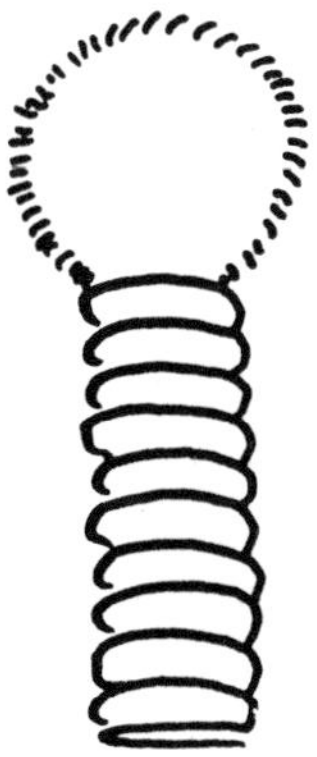

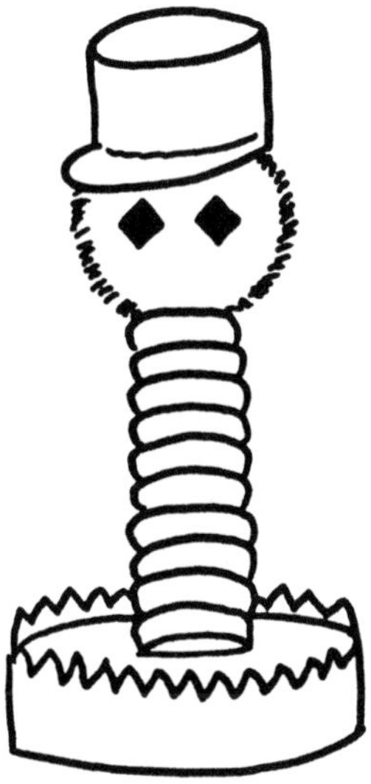

4. To make the base, cover the top of a small lid with black felt. Cut a strip of green felt, then cut the top edge into grass blades and glue the strip around the rim. Glue the bottom of the chenille stem spiral on top of the lid.

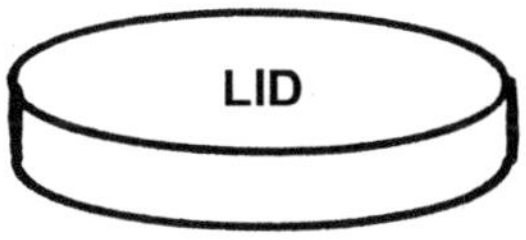

BRASS PICTURE FRAME

Mason jar lids are so beautiful that they shouldn't be used for canning alone. The rims just seem to be made for elegant frames to hold your school photos. Give one to your grandma!

You will need:

- ❑ Rim of the Mason jar lid
- ❑ 12" (30 cm) of ribbon
- ❑ Small brass ring
- ❑ Ruffled lace
- ❑ Tacky glue
- ❑ Scissors
- ❑ Rubber band
- ❑ Acetate sheet protector (to cover the photo)
- ❑ Stiff cardboard
- ❑ Photograph

What to do:

1. Insert the ribbon through the brass ring and then around top edge of the rim; tie ribbon ends together and make a knot behind the rim edge, out of sight.

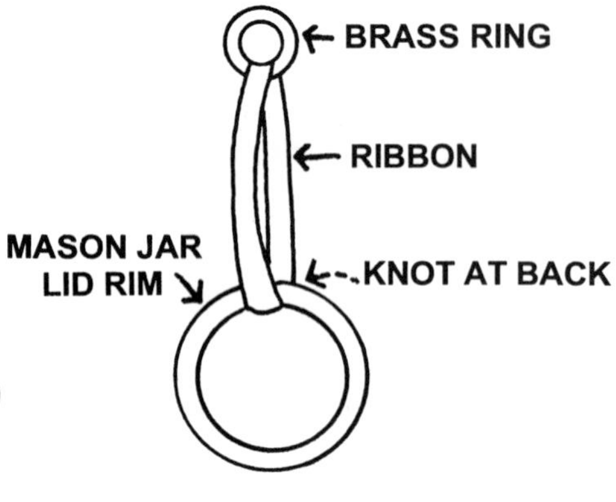

2. Glue ruffled lace all around the rim edge. (Push the ribbon to the back, out of the way.) Hold the lace in place with the rubber band until it is dry.

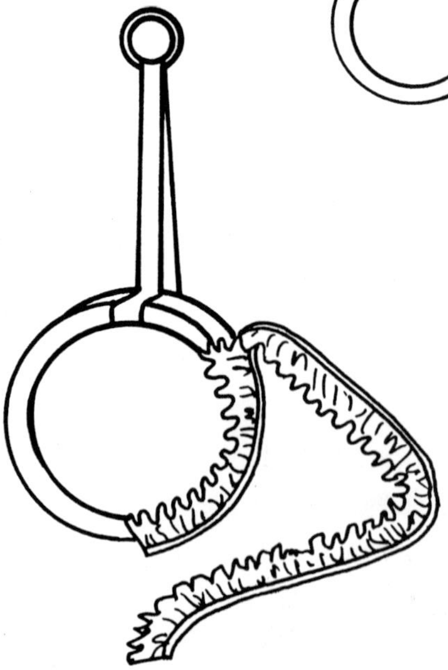

3. Cut a circle of acetate and a circle of cardboard to fit snugly inside the rim. Place the rim front side down on the table. Put the acetate circle in first, then cut your photo to fit, and place it (picture side down) on top of the acetate. Then place the cardboard circle on top, to hold the photo in place.

PURPLE CAT BOOKEND

A soft drink can is just the right size for a sturdy bookend. A purple cat is only one idea. I bet you will think of many other ways to decorate the can!

You will need:

- ❑ Empty soft drink can (washed and dried)
- ❑ Rice, dry beans or sand
- ❑ Masking tape
- ❑ Paper towel or toilet paper
- ❑ Tracing paper and pen
- ❑ Scissors
- ❑ Purple felt
- ❑ Black felt
- ❑ Yellow and turquoise felt scraps
- ❑ Tacky glue
- ❑ Black medium point permanent marker

What to do:

1. Fill the can with sand, rice or dry beans. Seal the opening securely with masking tape.

2. Cover the can top with crumpled paper towel or toilet paper to make it round. Stick long pieces of masking tape from one side of the can across the top to the other side. This will hold the paper top in place.

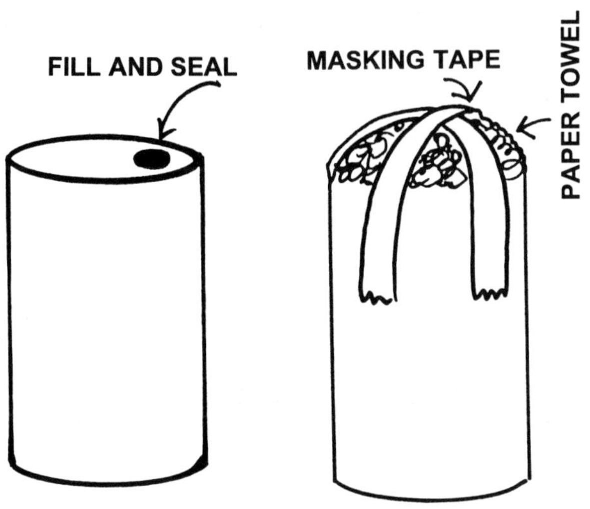

3. Cut a piece of purple felt, wide enough to go around the can and high enough to go from the can bottom to the top of the crumpled paper (7" x 9" or 18 cm x 23 cm). Using tacky glue, glue the felt on the can. Cut slits in the top edge and glue them down onto the top. (The slits help you to overlap the top edges to make it round and neat.)

4. Trace the pattern pieces onto tracing paper and cut them out. Cut smaller ears from the purple felt. Cut larger ears, nose and eyes from black felt. Cut eyes as shown from yellow and turquoise felt. Cut head top from black felt. Cut front edge into "hair", as shown. Glue the circle on the top of the can.

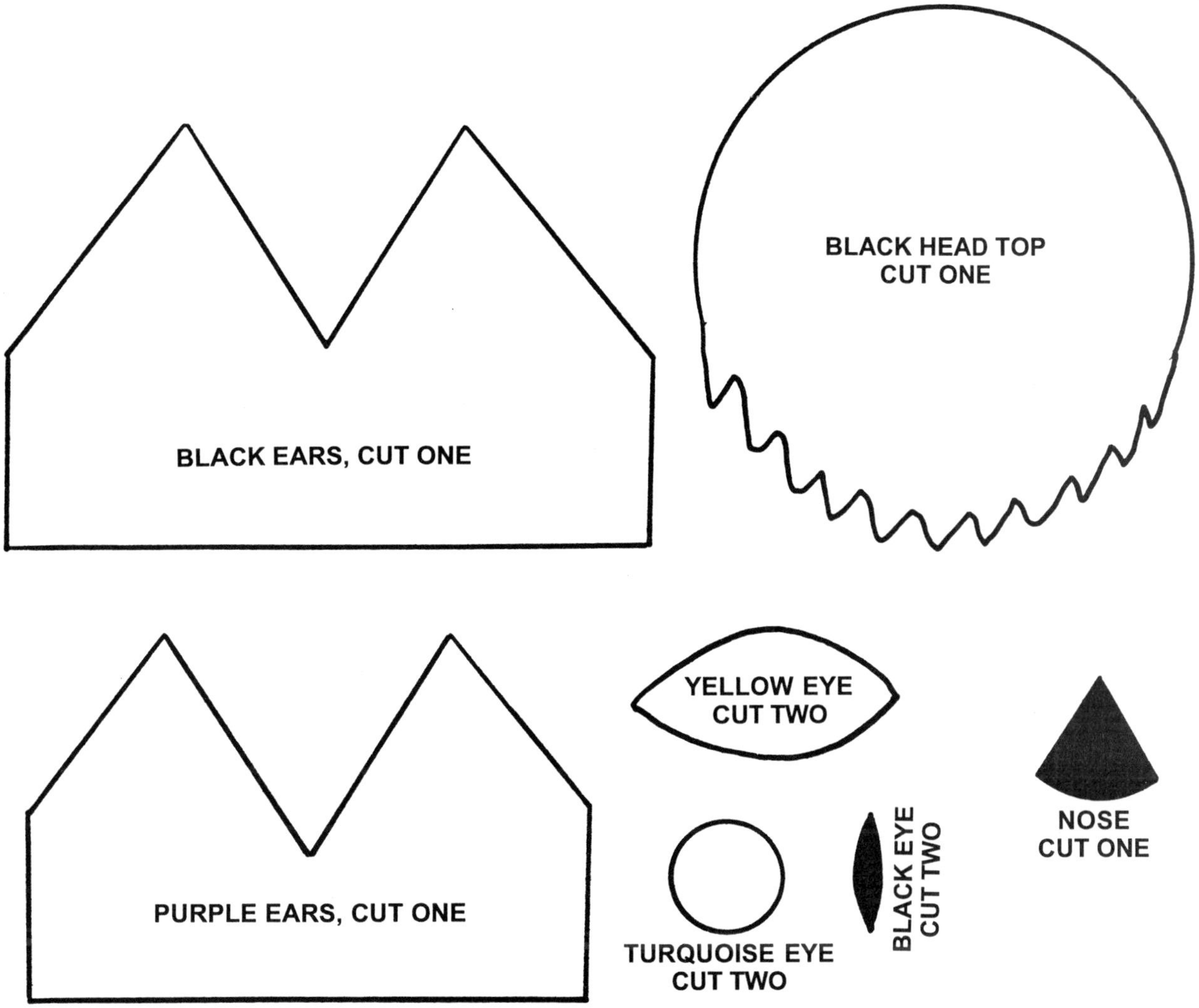

5. Glue the purple ears onto the black ones with lower edges even. Then glue the ears in place behind the top edge of the can.

6. Glue yellow eyes on the face, then turquoise pieces on top of the eyes and then the black pieces in the center of each eye. Glue the triangle nose in place.

7. Draw the mouth, whiskers, dots on the cheeks, paws and toes, as shown, with black marker.

KEEPSAKE BOOKMARKS

Bookmarks make wonderful little gifts for anyone who reads. Several ideas are shown here. Each bookmark becomes unique when you make it! If you have extras of small school photos from several grades, make a "me bookmark" for your grandparents. Look on the inside front cover for a sample of one that Rina made.

You will need:

- ❑ Tracing paper and pencil
- ❑ Scissors
- ❑ Thin cardboard or construction paper*
- ❑ Used stamps, magazine cutouts, cartoons, trip souvenirs (maps & brochures), photos, drawings
- ❑ Glue stick

Optional:

- ❑ Hole puncher
- ❑ 12" (30 cm) of narrow ribbon or cord

* Many magazines have large, white pieces of heavy paper (opposite ads, subscription forms or perfume samples). They are perfect for bookmarks.

What to do:

1. Cut a rectangular bookmark from thin cardboard or construction paper.

2. Select enough pretty stamps, colorful pictures from magazines, or souvenirs from your vacation to cover the cardboard. Arrange the pieces onto the front side of the bookmark and glue them in place. (See samples on next page for ideas.)

3. Write a message on back, like "Happy Birthday, Dad!"

4. If you want to add a ribbon, punch a hole at the top. Fold the ribbon in half. Push the loose ends through the hole from front to back (leaving the loop on the front side), and then push the loose ends through the center loop (twice, if necessary) and pull tight.

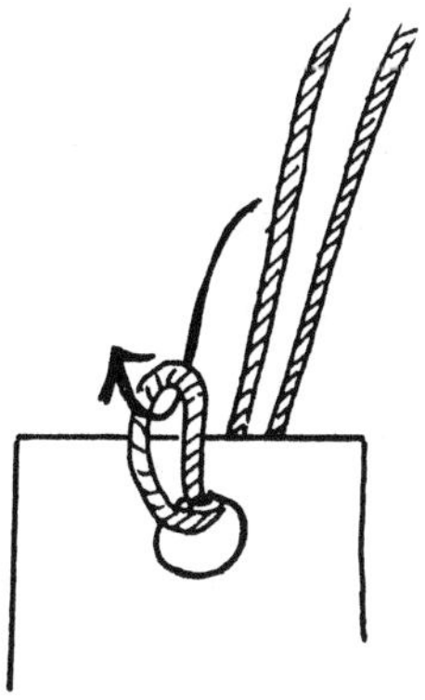

STAINED GLASS SUN CATCHER

Any dairy container with a tight lid makes a great snap-on frame. Make the "stained glass center" with ordinary wax crayon shavings and waxed paper.

You will need:

- ❑ Medium-sized plastic dairy container with lid (from yogurt, cottage cheese or sour cream)
- ❑ Scissors
- ❑ 15" (40 cm) of string (dental floss works well)
- ❑ Newspaper
- ❑ Waxed paper
- ❑ Potato peeler or pencil sharpener with large opening
- ❑ Wax crayons (use bright colors)
- ❑ Iron

What to do:

1. Make a frame from the dairy container by cutting out the lid's center, keeping only the rim. Then cut off the lower part of the container, keeping only the rim.

2. Tie a piece of string around the lid rim to make a loop for hanging.

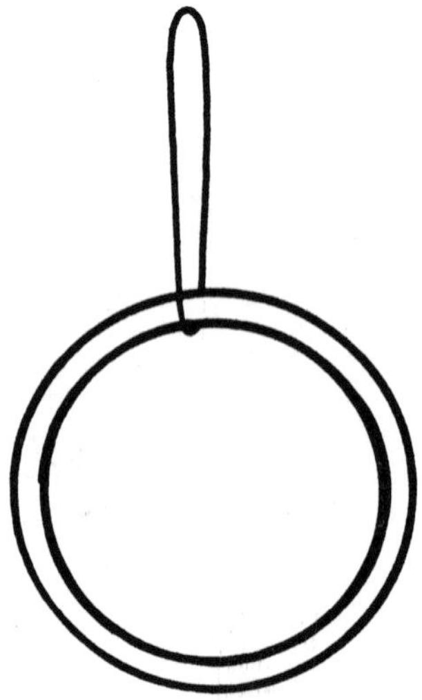

3. Put several sheets of newspaper on an ironing board (to protect the board). Put a sheet of waxed paper (shiny side up) on top of the newspaper. Use a potato peeler or pencil sharpener to shave old crayons. Spread the shavings generously on the waxed paper, mixing the colors into a nice pattern.

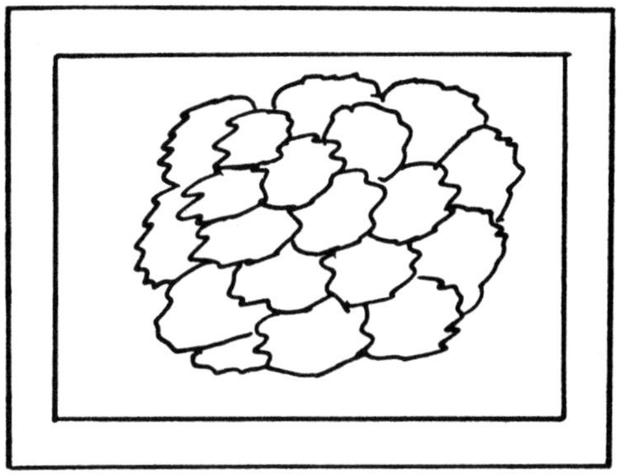

4. Put another sheet of waxed paper on top of the shavings, shiny side down. Place two more sheets of newspaper on top to protect your iron from wax. Ask an adult to press with a warm iron, a few seconds at a time, until the crayon shavings melt (but do not burn them!) and the waxed paper layers are sealed together.

5. Put the sealed waxed sheets between the two rims and snap the rims together. Trim excess waxed paper from around the edges as closely as possible. Be careful not to cut the string. Hang it in the window.

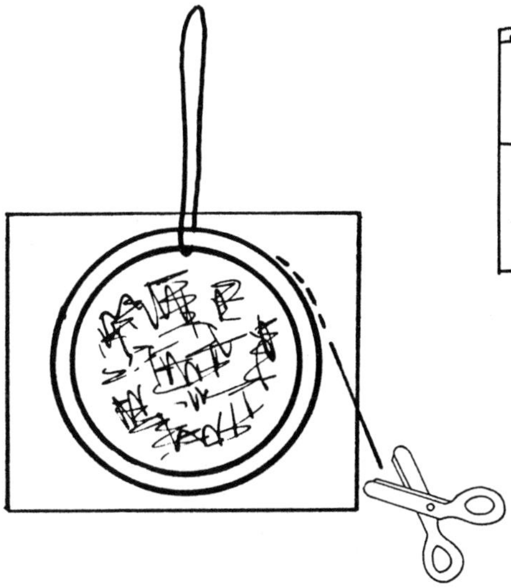

MAGAZINE BIN

This handy container holds magazines, books or other papers upright. It also makes a great wastepaper basket. You can use this idea to make containers of any size for all occasions. You can go wild decorating it depending on the person who will get it.

You will need:

- ❑ Large, sturdy plastic or cardboard container with square bottom, wide enough for magazines (from laundry detergent, spring water, cat litter, etc.)
- ❑ Scissors
- ❑ Colorful tissue paper, old telephone directory pages, cartoon strips, etc.
- ❑ Decoupage paste and brush

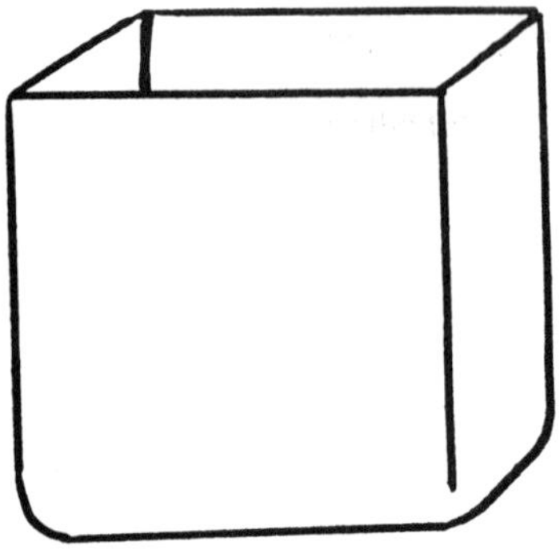

What to do:

1. Ask a grownup to cut off the top of the container. You'll want to keep the bottom part about 8" (20 cm) high. Wash and dry the bottom part well.

2. Tear or cut colorful tissue paper, telephone directory pages, cartoon strips, magazine pictures, or souvenirs from travel brochures into small pieces. Brush decoupage paste on the outside of the container, a small section at a time, and paste the paper pieces all over, overlapping the edges. Continue until the surface is covered. Brush more paste on top.

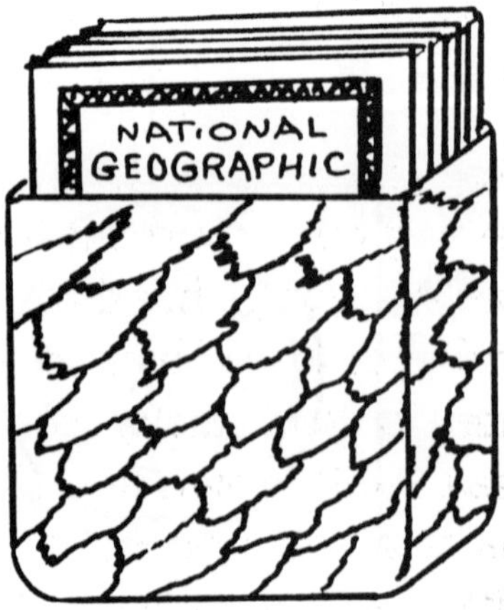

3. Let dry well.

SPY BIRDIE

This little bird perches on top of a cork and watches you. Your friends will love it!

You will need:

- ❑ Cork (from wine bottle)
- ❑ Scissors
- ❑ Red wooden bead for body, 1" (2.5 cm)
- ❑ Red wooden bead for head, 3/4" (2 cm)
- ❑ Carpenter's glue
- ❑ Tracing paper and pen
- ❑ Tacky glue
- ❑ Black felt scraps
- ❑ Light brown felt scrap

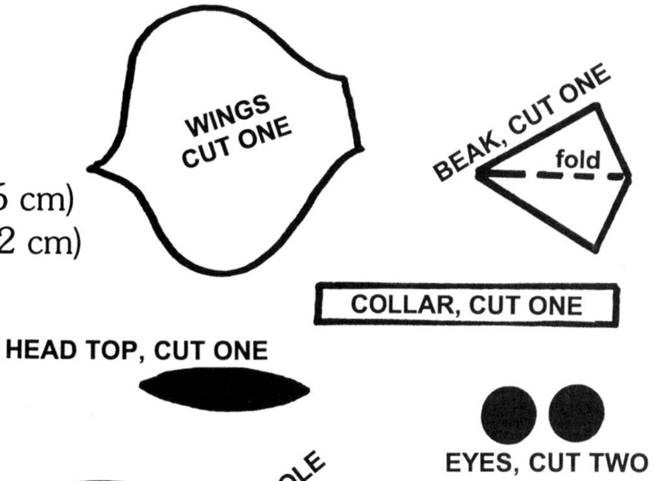

What to do:

1. Hollow out the cork top about 1/4" (6 mm) deep with the tip of the scissors, as shown with the broken line in the illustration.

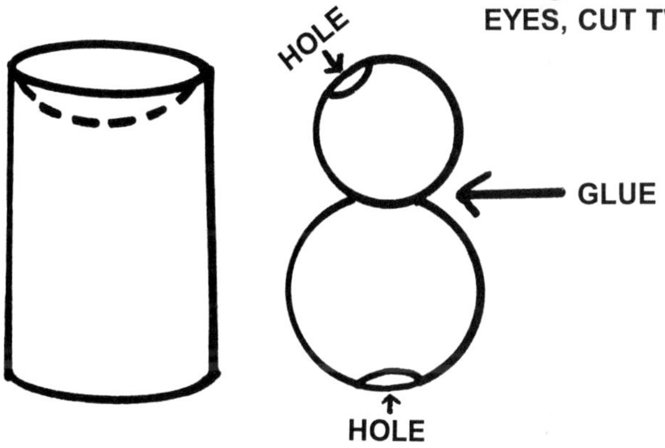

2. Glue the two beads together with carpenter's glue, as shown. Let dry well.

3. Glue the bottom of the body bead onto the cork top with tacky glue. (The bird leans forward.)

4. Trace the patterns onto tracing paper and cut them out. Cut the wings, head top, collar and eyes from black felt and glue them on with tacky glue. Cut the beak from brown felt. Pinch it to make a sharp peak, as shown with the broken line. Glue it on the face.

GOLDEN JAR

This jar is made with golden glitter but you may also use silver, green, blue, red... Fill the jar with bath oil beads, smooth pebbles, seashells, potpourri, cotton balls or dried flowers with stems. This is particularly lovely for Mother's Day or Mom's birthday. (See page 17 for directions to make potpourri.)

You will need:

- ❑ Straight glass jar with wide mouth (from salsa, peanut butter, etc.)
- ❑ White liquid glue and brush
- ❑ Gold sparkle glitter
- ❑ Waxed paper
- ❑ Ribbon

What to do:

1. Brush white liquid glue generously all over the outside of the jar, but not on the rim.

2. While the glue is still wet, sprinkle gold glitter on the jar until it is evenly coated. Hold the jar over a sheet of waxed paper so you can reuse the glitter that falls off.

3. Let dry thoroughly. Brush white liquid glue on top of the glitter to seal it and let dry again until the glue becomes transparent. (If the glue is too thick, first dilute it with a bit of water in a small bowl.)

4. Tie a beautiful ribbon around the rim and make a bow.

MINI MEMO BOARD

Styrofoam trays usually end up in the trash. Rescue a few of them to make a memo board for important notes.

You will need:

- ❑ Three small styrofoam trays from meat or vegetables, washed well
- ❑ Scissors or dull knife
- ❑ Aluminum foil
- ❑ Nail or toothpick
- ❑ 20” (50 cm) of cord
- ❑ Push pins

What to do:

1. Cut the raised edges off the trays because you only need the flat middle part.

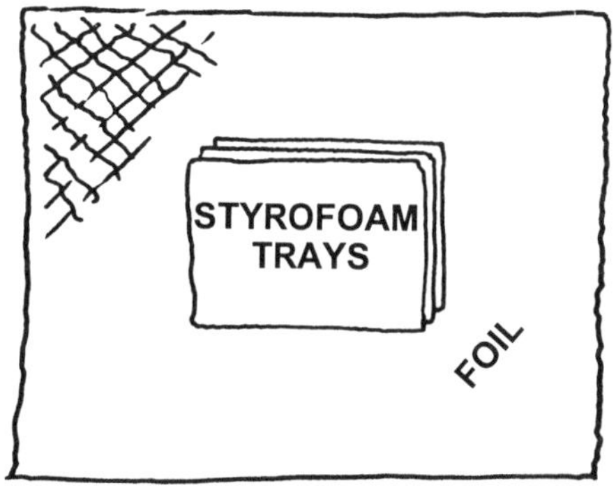

2. Stack all three trays on top of one another. Crinkle a large sheet of foil slightly, then straighten it out and wrap it tightly and neatly around the trays, hiding the ends at the back. Crinkling makes the foil stronger and gives it an interesting texture.

3. Punch two small holes in the upper edge with a nail or a toothpick and push a cord through the holes for hanging. Tie the cord ends together at the back, out of sight.

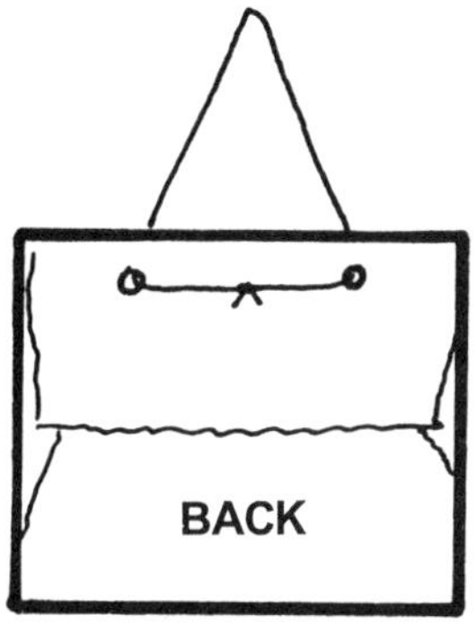

4. Add a few pushpins and the first memo such as “Happy Birthday, Michelle!”.

FRAMED MAGNET

Collect small lids to make neat frames for magnets. Use stickers, photos or magazine cutouts in the frame. Or make your own picture from construction paper scraps.

You will need:

- ❑ Small lid, 2-3" (5-8 cm) wide
- ❑ Photo, magazine cutout or sticker
- ❑ Glue stick
- ❑ Scissors
- ❑ Self-adhesive magnetic strip
- ❑ Cord or ribbon for decoration (optional)

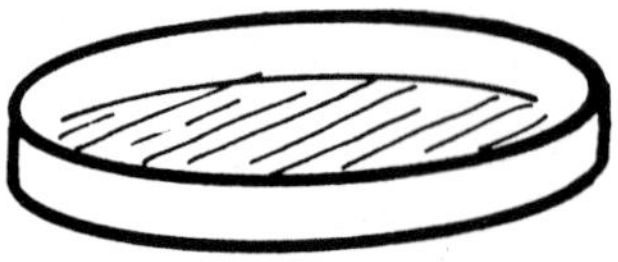

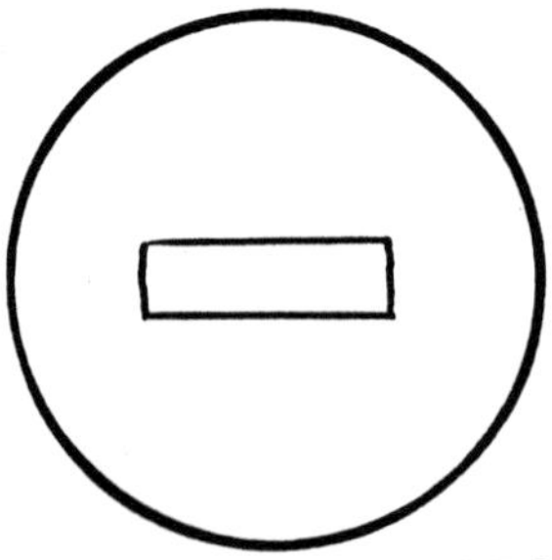

MAGNETIC STRIP ON BACK

What to do:

1. Cut a photo of yourself or your pet, or a magazine picture, to fit inside the lid and glue it in place.

2. Stick a piece of self-adhesive magnetic strip on the back.

3. If you wish, glue a piece of cord around the inside rim. Or add a ribbon around the outside rim; tie the ribbon into a bow at the bottom.

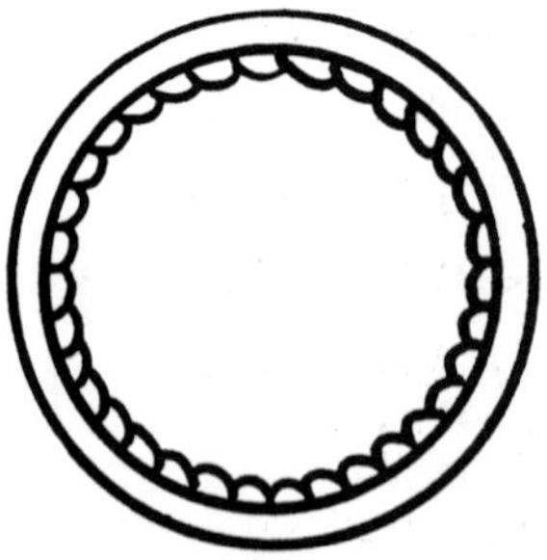

CORD INSIDE THE RIM

RIBBON AROUND THE RIM

PEN & PENCIL KEEPER

Everyone uses pens and they must put them somewhere! Your teenage sister or brother, teacher or parent will find this container handy and attractive.

You will need:

❑ Empty soup can
❑ Construction paper scraps (3 or 4 different colors)
❑ White liquid glue and brush

What to do:

1. Wash and dry the can, and remove the label. (Make sure the cut edge is smooth. If there's a rough spot, press it flat with a wooden spoon handle or pliers so that it will not cut anyone.)

2. Tear different colors of construction paper into small roundish pieces (about 1" or 2.5 cm). Starting from the top edge, brush glue on the outside of the can, a small section at a time, and glue the pieces all over, overlapping the edges. Alternate the colors to make a nice pattern. Use straight paper edges along top and bottom. Continue until the surface is covered.

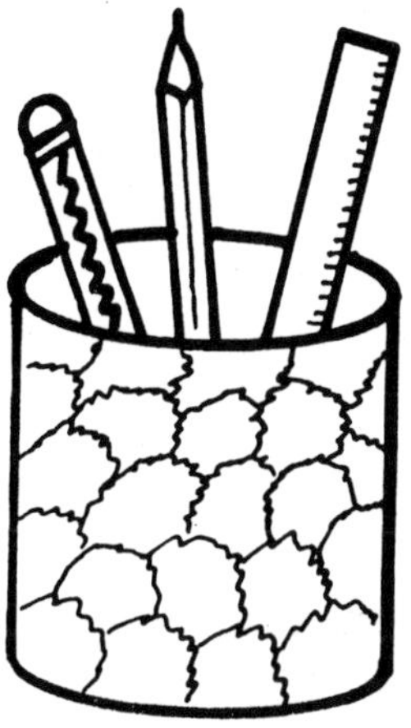

3. Brush more glue on top. Dilute the glue first with a bit of water if it is very thick. Let dry thoroughly.

LADYBUG PAPERWEIGHT

This makes a conversation piece on your parent's desk. The ladybug is so shiny and red that it looks good enough to eat, but it's just a styrofoam ball covered with tissue paper and glossy decoupage paste. It makes a good paperweight and an equally attractive decoration.

You will need:

- ❑ Large tuna can (washed and dried); also keep the loose lid
- ❑ Rock (to fit into the tuna can)
- ❑ Sand or toilet paper
- ❑ Masking tape
- ❑ Green felt
- ❑ Scissors
- ❑ Black crayon
- ❑ Tacky glue
- ❑ Blunt knife
- ❑ 3" (8 cm) styrofoam ball
- ❑ 1" (2.5 cm) styrofoam ball
- ❑ Three toothpicks
- ❑ Red and black tissue paper
- ❑ Glossy decoupage paste and brush
- ❑ Black and white felt scraps
- ❑ Black chenille stem

What to do:

1. Put the rock into the can and fill any empty space around the rock with sand or toilet paper. Cover with loose lid and tape the lid in place with masking tape, wrapping the tape securely all around.

2. Cut two circles from green felt to cover the top and bottom of the can. (To cut the circles, trace the can bottom directly onto the felt with black crayon.) Glue the circles in place.

3. Cut a green felt strip 10 1/2" long x 2 1/2" wide (27 cm x 6.5 cm). Cut one long top edge into grass blades, as shown. Glue the strip around the can, bottom edges even and grass blades sticking upward over the top edge. (Felt is fragile when it's cut into "grass blades" so do not pull or tear it.)

4. Cut both styrofoam balls in half with a blunt knife. (You will only need half of each ball; the larger one is the body and the smaller one is the head.) Carve a small hole in the bottom front of the body for the head. Push the head into the indentation in the front of the body. Attach it tightly in place with two toothpicks, pushing the picks through both the head and body until out of sight.

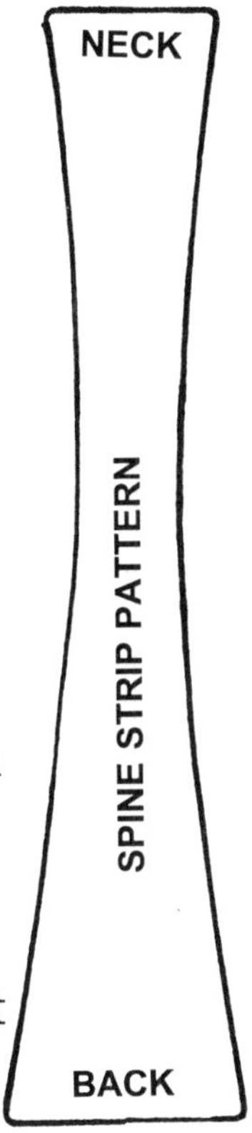

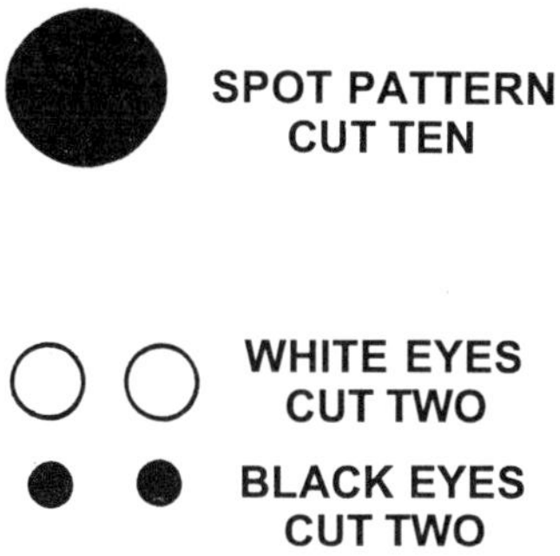

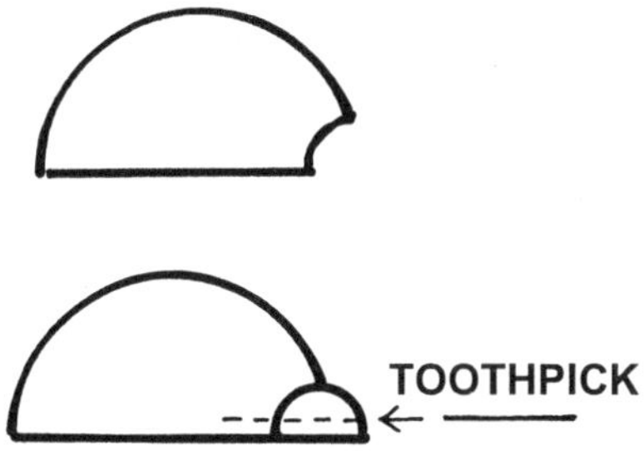

5. Tear little pieces of red tissue paper and a few tiny pieces of black tissue paper. Brush decoupage paste all over the ladybug's back and paste pieces of red paper all around, overlapping the pieces. Continue covering until there are two or three coats of paper. (It will look pink until the paste dries and then the bug will be bright red.) Cover the head with black pieces of paper. Brush more paste on top. Let dry overnight.

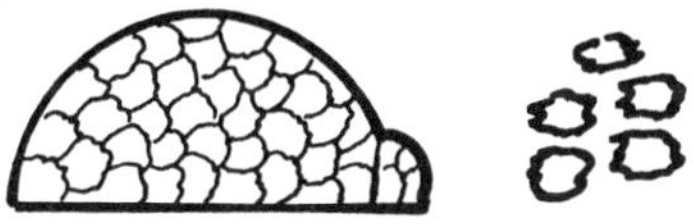

6. With tacky glue, glue the bottom of the ladybug onto the top of the can.

7. Cut small circles from white felt and glue them on for eyes. Glue tiny black felt circles on the white ones. Cut two pieces from black chenille stem (1 1/2" or 4 cm each) to make antennae and bend upper ends down. Poke small holes for antennae using the remaining toothpick, fill holes with tacky glue and push antenna ends into the holes.

8. Cut a strip of black felt and glue it along the spine, as shown (wide end at bottom back and narrow end at neck). Cut ten black felt circles and glue them on the back.

FOUR-HEART CARD

This card is perfect for Valentine's Day, Mother's Day or Father's Day. It is very simple to make and you can decorate it any way you like.

You will need:

- ❑ Tracing paper and pencil
- ❑ Scissors
- ❑ Sheet of white typing paper, 8 1/2" x 11" (22 cm x 28 cm)
- ❑ Markers

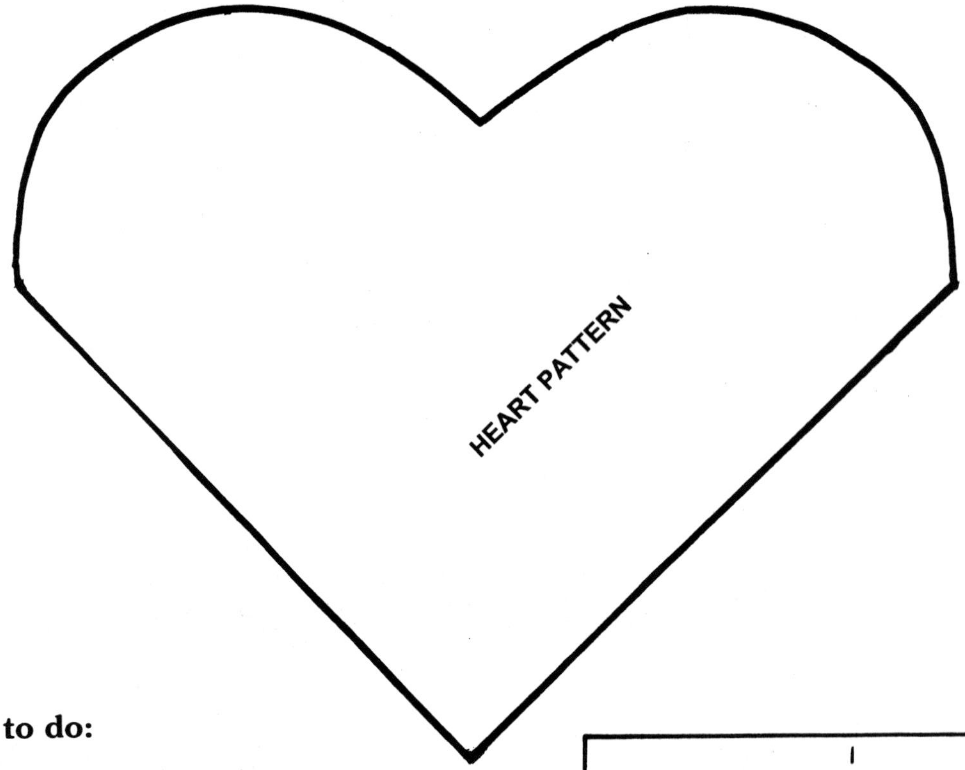

What to do:

1. Trace the heart pattern onto tracing paper and cut it out.

2. Fold a sheet of typing paper in half. Then fold it in half again, as shown. The card now has four layers.

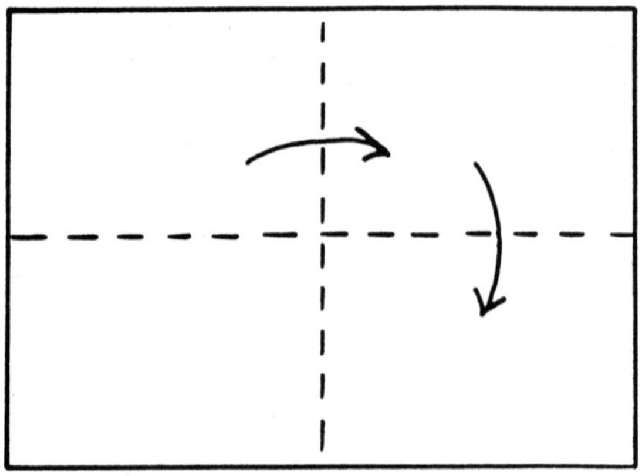

3. Trace the heart pattern, as shown, onto the folded card, with corners and edges matching. Cut the heart out and discard the extra paper.

4. Unfold the card and you'll have four hearts together. Decorate the sections with bright markers inside and outside.

ROCKY BOOKMARK

This large, colorful bookmark is amazingly simple, yet so artistic with a rainbow of "Rocky Mountains". You probably have a stack of construction paper in your room, so you can make this bookmark anytime you need a little gift for someone nice.

You will need:

- ❑ Construction paper (yellow, red, purple, green)
- ❑ Scissors
- ❑ Glue stick
- ❑ Ruler, pencil
- ❑ Black marker

What to do:

1. Cut a 3 1/2" x 8 1/4" (9 cm x 21 cm) piece of construction paper in each of the four colors. Rip the upper edges of the red, purple and green pieces.

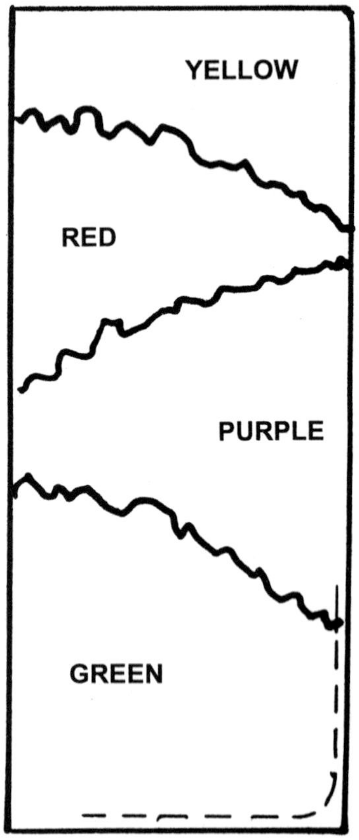

2. Glue the red paper on the yellow, then put the purple in the middle, then put the green at the bottom. Cut off the lower edges so that all the layers are even with the yellow one. (Do not worry if the edges are not very neat; they will be trimmed later.)

3. On the back, draw straight cutting lines all around using a ruler and pencil. Cut the bookmark out and round off the corners.

4. Write a message with black marker.

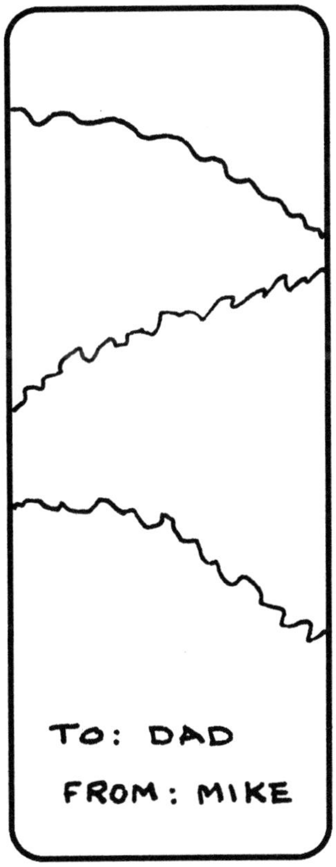
TO: DAD
FROM: MIKE

BOOKMARK PATTERN
(cut four in different colors)

EASTER BUNNY BASKET

This is a very simple and fast idea. Any candy will taste delicious in the bunny basket! Make this for someone who has a sweet tooth — your teacher, brothers and sisters, friends or grandpa.

You will need:

- ❑ Tracing paper and pencil
- ❑ Scissors
- ❑ Yellow and purple construction paper
- ❑ Plastic container or can, 3" (8 cm) wide
- ❑ Glue stick
- ❑ Black marker
- ❑ Cotton ball
- ❑ Jelly beans or other candies

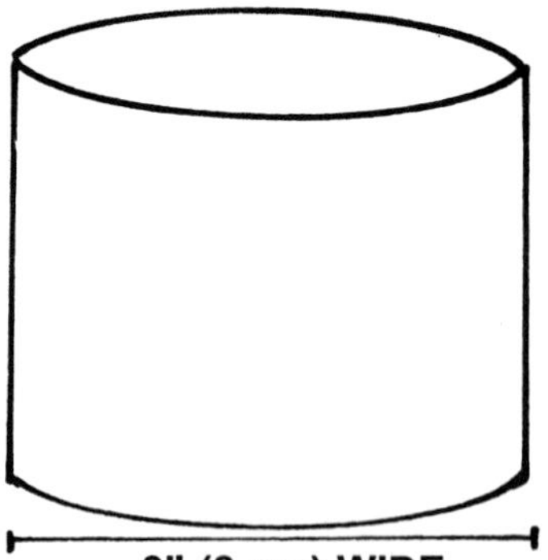

What to do:

1. Trace the bunny and paw patterns onto tracing paper and cut them out.

2. Trace the bunny and two paws onto yellow construction paper and cut them out. Draw the face with the black marker.

3. Glue purple construction paper all around the can.

4. Glue the can onto the bunny's tummy, wrap the arms around to the front and glue them in place. Glue the paws to the front edge, as shown.

5. Glue the cotton ball tail to the bottom back.

6. Fill the can with Easter candies.

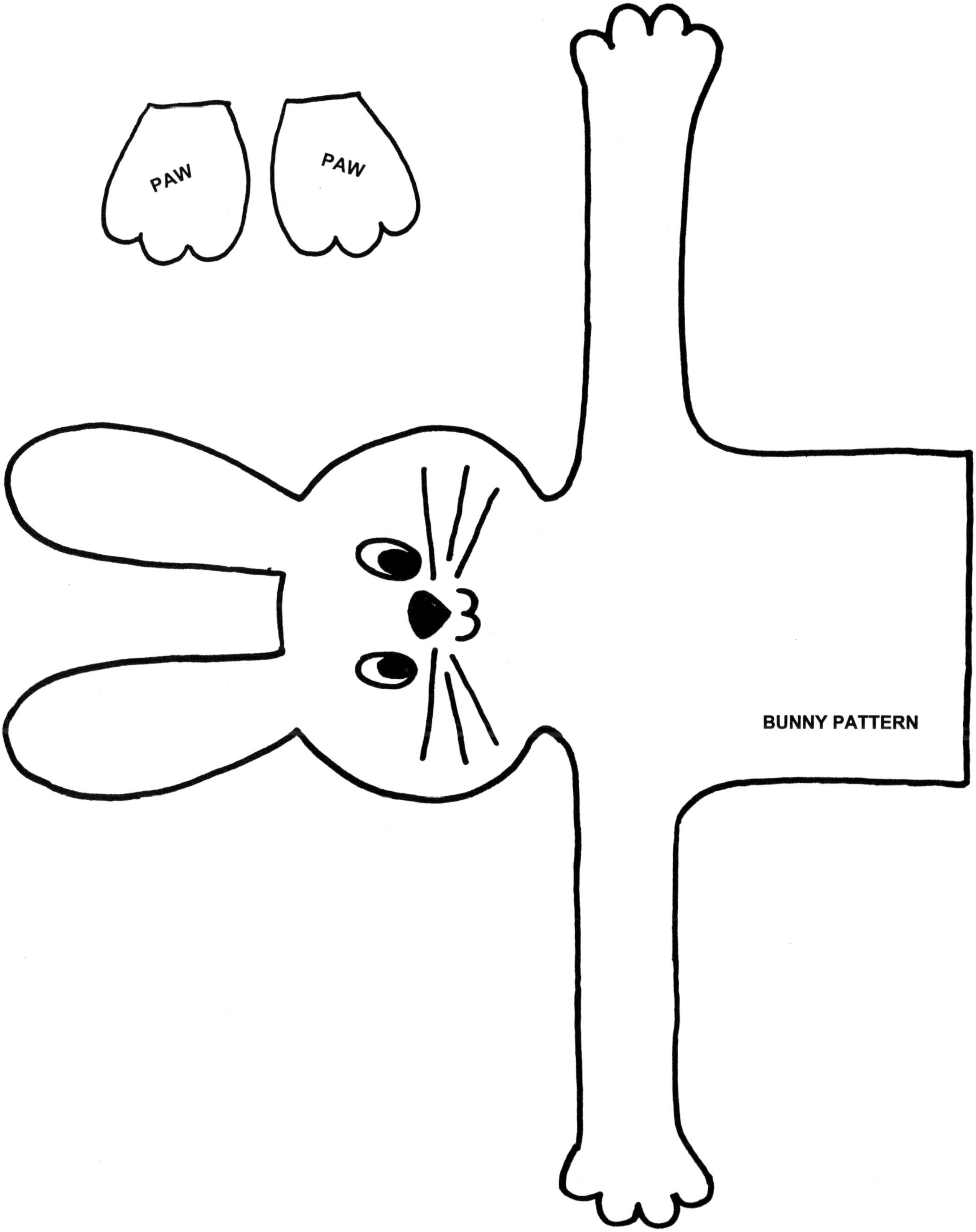
PAW
PAW
BUNNY PATTERN

EASTER PIÑATA

All kids love to work with papier-mâché! Use a balloon to make a beautiful paper ball and hide candies or toys in it. A quick snip of the scissors cuts off one end to reveal the surprises. (Please note that this gift takes several days to make since it must dry overnight between each layer.)

You will need:

- ❑ Medium-sized round balloon
- ❑ String
- ❑ Newspapers
- ❑ White liquid glue and water
- ❑ Old tablespoon for measuring
- ❑ Small bowl for glue
- ❑ Bowl to hold the balloon
- ❑ Brush for glue
- ❑ Tissue paper in assorted colors (for example, yellow, green and blue)
- ❑ Scissors
- ❑ Wrapped candy

What to do:

1. Blow up the balloon and tie it with a string. Do not cut the string ends.

2. Protect your tabletop with newspapers. In a small bowl, dilute six tablespoons of white liquid glue with three tablespoons of water. (Make more glue as needed.)

3. Tear off small pieces of tissue paper. Brush diluted glue over the balloon, a small section at a time, and paste on the paper pieces. Overlap the pieces and brush more glue on top. Continue to cover the balloon, making large patches of different colors, overlapping them at edges. Hold the balloon in empty bowl while you work so that it won't roll all over the place. Leave a 2" (5 cm) patch uncovered around the knot. Then turn the balloon right side up, knotted end down, and cover the top.

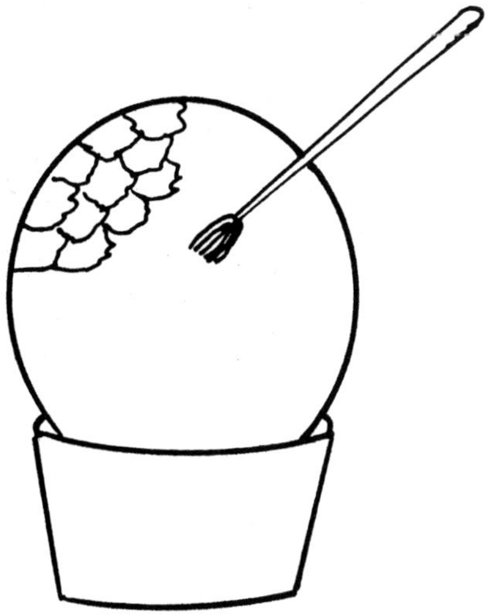

4. Use the string to hang the balloon upside down. Let dry overnight.

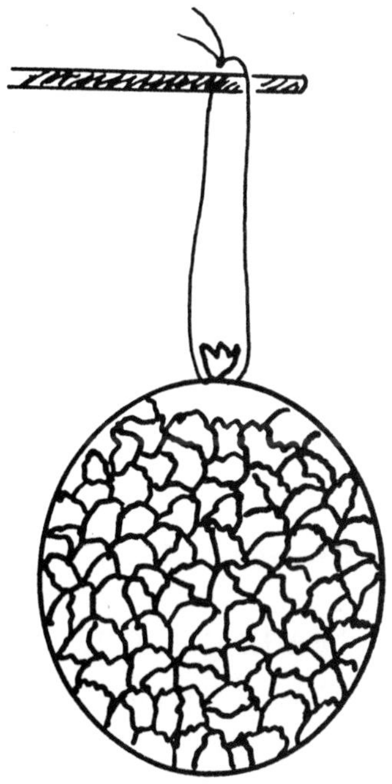

5. Paste two more layers of paper pieces on the balloon, letting it dry overnight between each layer. You will now have three layers.

6. Cut the knotted end off, pull the balloon out and discard it.

7. Fill the Piñata with wrapped candies.

8. Paste tissue paper pieces to cover the opening. Let dry. Repeat until you have three layers.

SNOWFLAKE ANGEL

This lovely angel, made of white onionskin paper, is elegant and festive. Hang it in the window or on Christmas tree. Make a mobile out of several angels! Each angel can be different, depending on how you cut it. See samples on inside back cover. (If you want to mail this gift in an envelope, do not glue wings to skirt or stickers on face. Mail it folded and cut, and include instructions on how to finish it.)

You will need:

- ❑ Sheet of white onionskin paper 8 1/2" x 11" (22 cm x 28 cm)
- ❑ Scissors
- ❑ Small piece of string for neck
- ❑ 12" (30 cm) of cord for hanging
- ❑ Glue stick
- ❑ White liquid glue
- ❑ Two stickers of angel face (or angel faces cut from a magazine)

What to do:

1. Starting at one end, pleat the paper in 1/2" (13 mm) folds, accordion style.

2. Press the pleats together tightly. Cut through all layers to make a "neck", as shown. (Be careful not to cut all the way through.) Tie a piece of string around the neck and cut ends off.

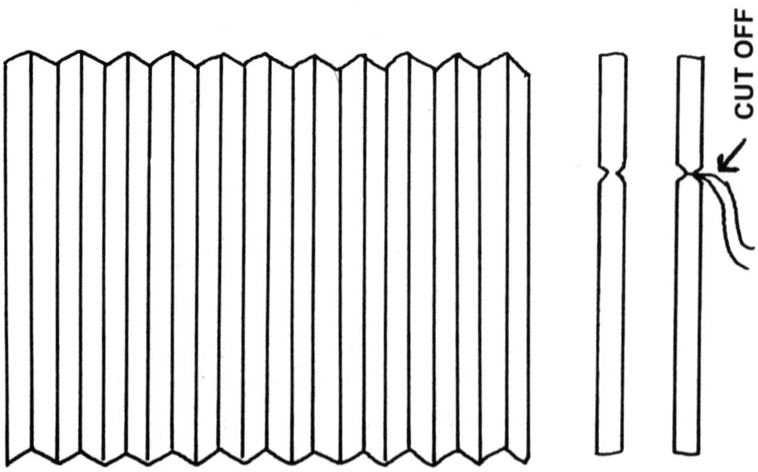

3. Three full-size patterns are shown here or create your own design. Cut both ends, through all layers, as shown. Decorate wings and skirt by cutting both edges, through all layers, as shown.

4. Gently open the pleats. Using the glue stick, glue the wing edges to skirt edges at each side.

5. Tie the cord on top for hanging.

6. Glue a sticker of an angel face on each side with white liquid glue.

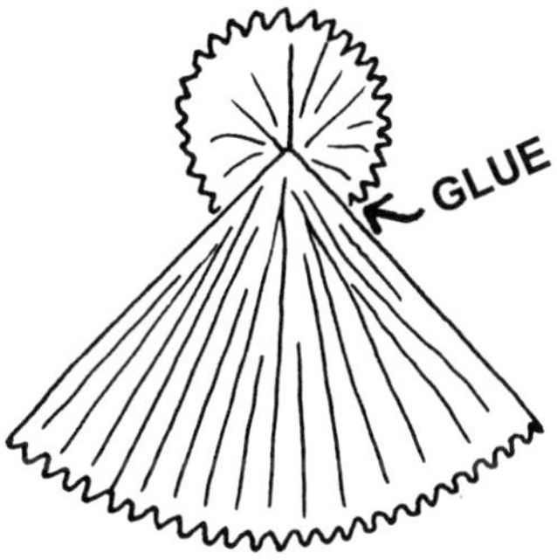

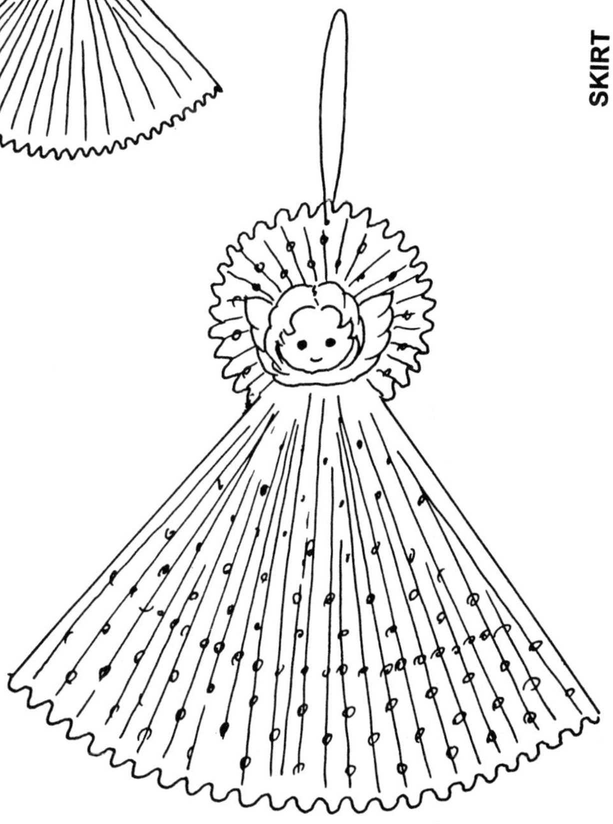

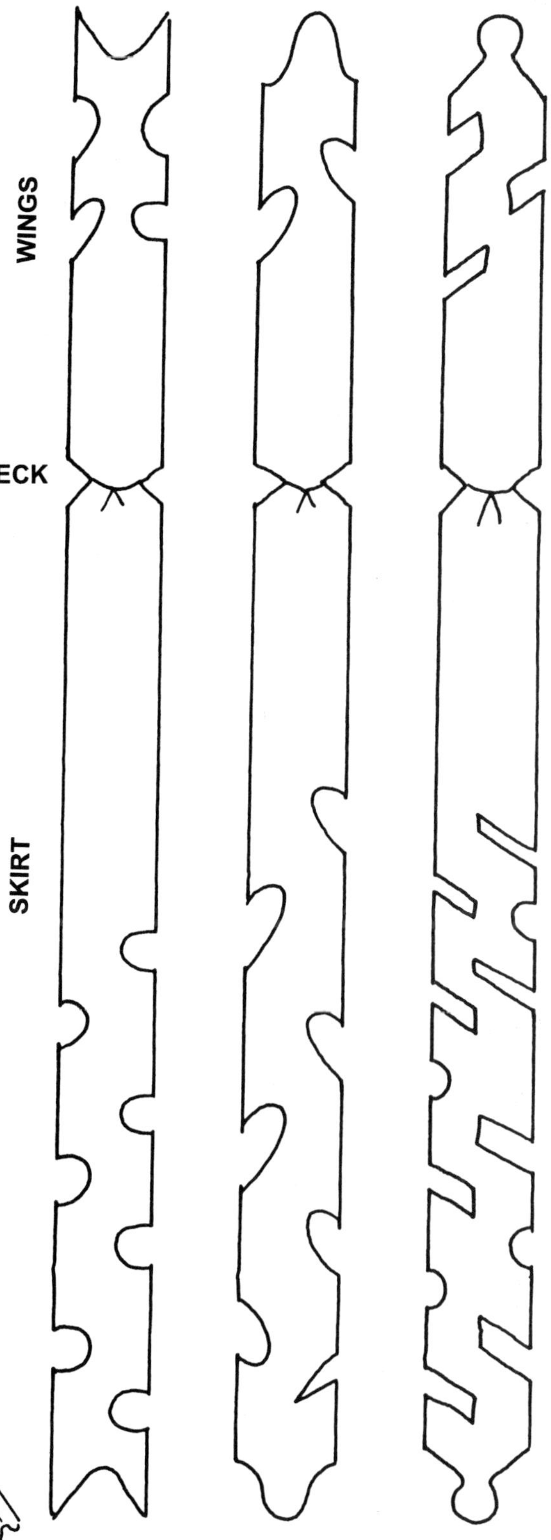

BIGFOOT GNOME

This gnome has big button feet so he can stand on a tabletop. You can twist and turn the arms and legs.

You will need:

- ❑ Wooden bead for head, natural color, 1" (2.5 cm)
- ❑ Two red wooden beads for body, 1/2" (13 mm)
- ❑ 15 red wooden beads for legs, arms and head top, 1/3" (8 mm)
- ❑ Four red chenille stems
- ❑ Two flat, black buttons, 1 1/2" (4 cm) wide, with four holes each
- ❑ Tracing paper and pen
- ❑ Scissors
- ❑ Red felt for hat
- ❑ Tiny jingle bell or liberty bell
- ❑ 4" (10 cm) of red string
- ❑ Tacky glue
- ❑ Black fine point permanent marker

What to do:

1. Twist the four chenille stems together 1/3 of the way from top, as shown.

2. Divide the top four chenille stems, as shown (one arm on each side and two for head).

3. Body: Push all four lower chenille stems through two medium-sized beads to make the body.

4. Arms and hands: Push each arm into three small beads. Turn the chenille stem at each arm's end backward into a tiny loop for a hand and twist loose end around the wrist.

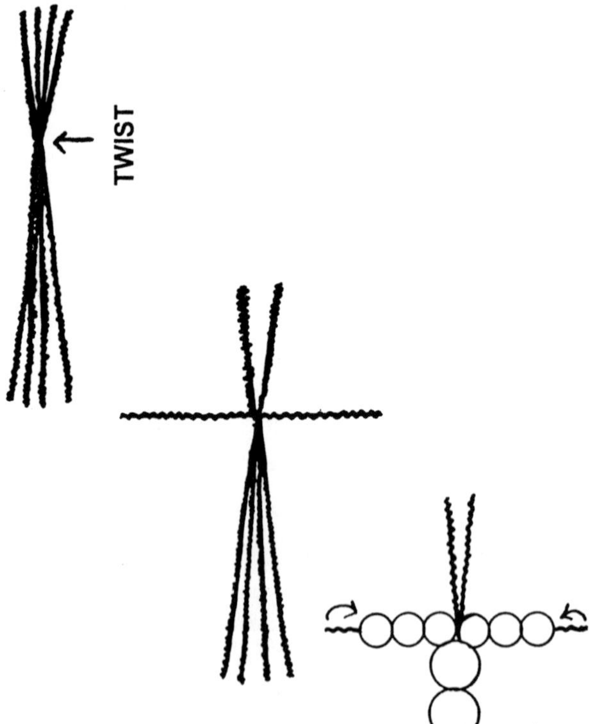

5. Legs and feet: Divide the four lower chenille stems into two legs. Push each leg into four small beads. Attach each leg to a button by pushing each chenille stem through a separate hole, and then backward through the two remaining holes. Twist the stem ends tightly around the ankle.

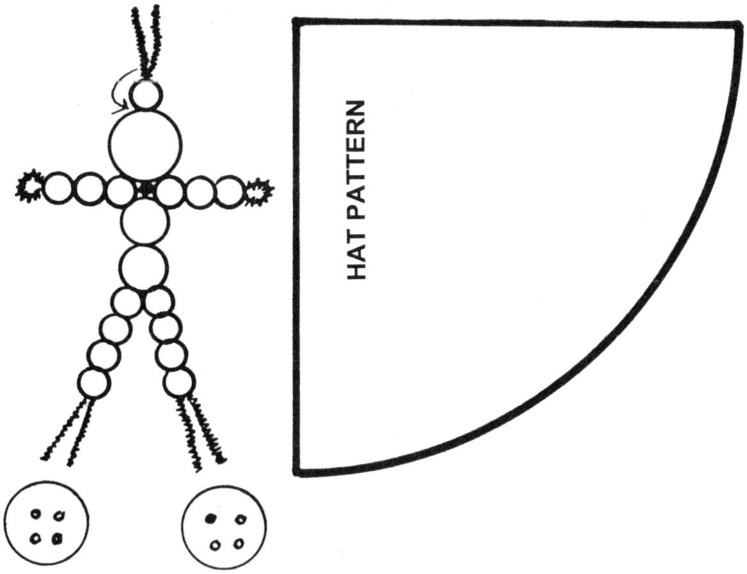

6. Head: Push the two remaining chenille stems on the top through the large natural color bead, then through one remaining small bead, then twist and wrap the chenille stem ends between the two beads. This will hold the head securely in place.

7. Hat: Trace the hat pattern onto tracing paper and cut it out. Trace the pattern onto red felt and cut it out. Push the string through the jingle bell and make a knot below the bell. Glue string ends to the back inside edge of the hat. Overlap the back edges and glue them together to make a cone hat. Spread glue around the head bead and glue the hat on.

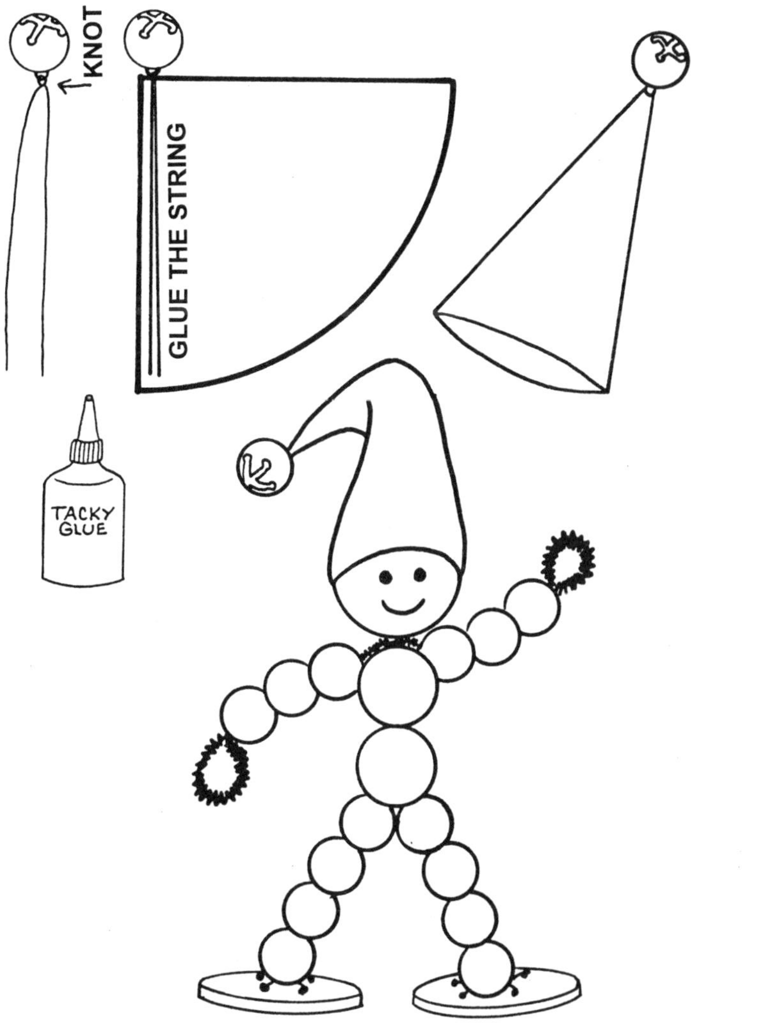

8. Face: Draw eyes and mouth with the black marker.

CRANBERRY CLUSTER

This pretty ornament for the Christmas tree is easy to make and costs only pennies.

You will need:

- ❑ Toilet paper tube
- ❑ Scissors
- ❑ Green crepe paper
- ❑ Double-sided tape
- ❑ Three red wooden beads, 1/2" (13 mm) each
- ❑ Tinsel stem (metallic pipe cleaner)
- ❑ Nail
- ❑ Red curling ribbon

What to do:

1. Cut 1" (2.5 cm) wide ring from toilet paper tube.

2. Cut 1/2" (13 mm) wide strips of crepe paper and wrap them tightly around the ring, around and around at a slight angle, completely covering the ring. Hold the paper in place at each end with double-sided tape.

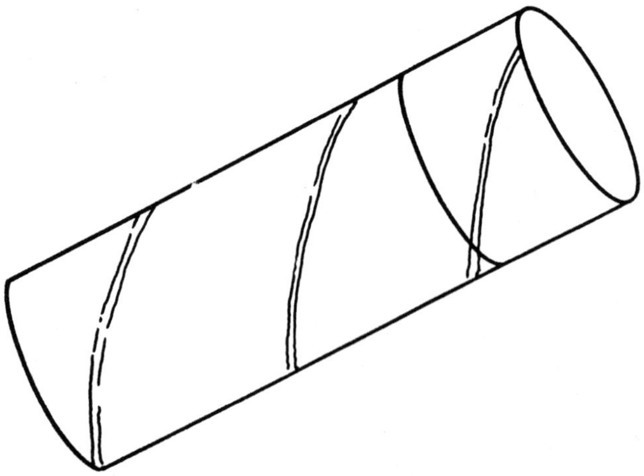

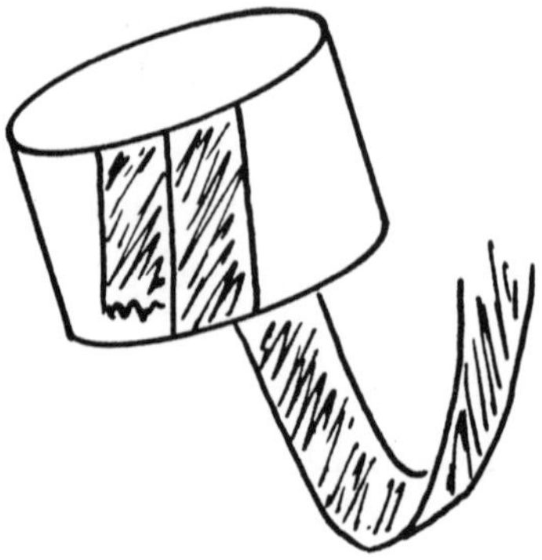

3. Push the tinsel stem through three red wooden beads. Bring ends together forming a triangle with the beads so that one tinsel stem end is only 1" (2.5 cm) long. Twist the tinsel stems together on top of wooden beads.

4. Use a nail to poke a tiny hole through the cardboard ring, center top. Push the tinsel stem ends through the hole, from inside to outside, pull tight and twist. Turn the longer tinsel stem end into a loop for hanging and twist the ends together.

5. Tie the red curling ribbon around the ring, on the outside center, into a bow at the top. Curl the ribbon ends.

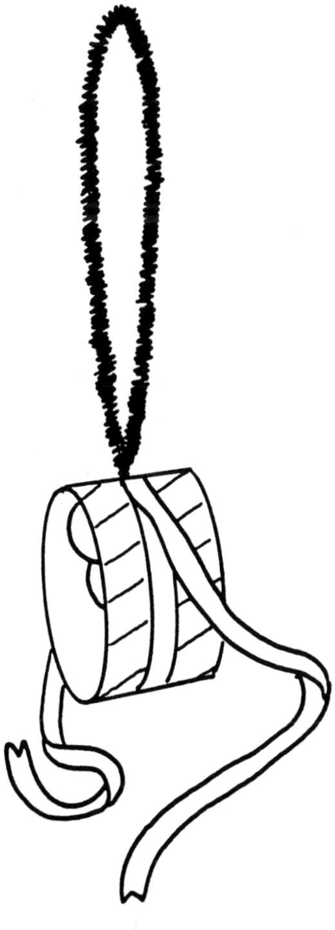

RICEBAG SANTA

Make several happy Santas to give to your friends and relatives. They will keep them year after year! It requires a little bit of sewing to close the edges but it is very easy.

You will need:

- ❑ Tracing paper and pen
- ❑ Scissors
- ❑ Red felt
- ❑ White and black felt scraps
- ❑ Medium-sized jingle bell or liberty bell
- ❑ Red chenille stem
- ❑ Tacky glue
- ❑ Darning needle and red yarn
- ❑ Three tablespoons of uncooked rice

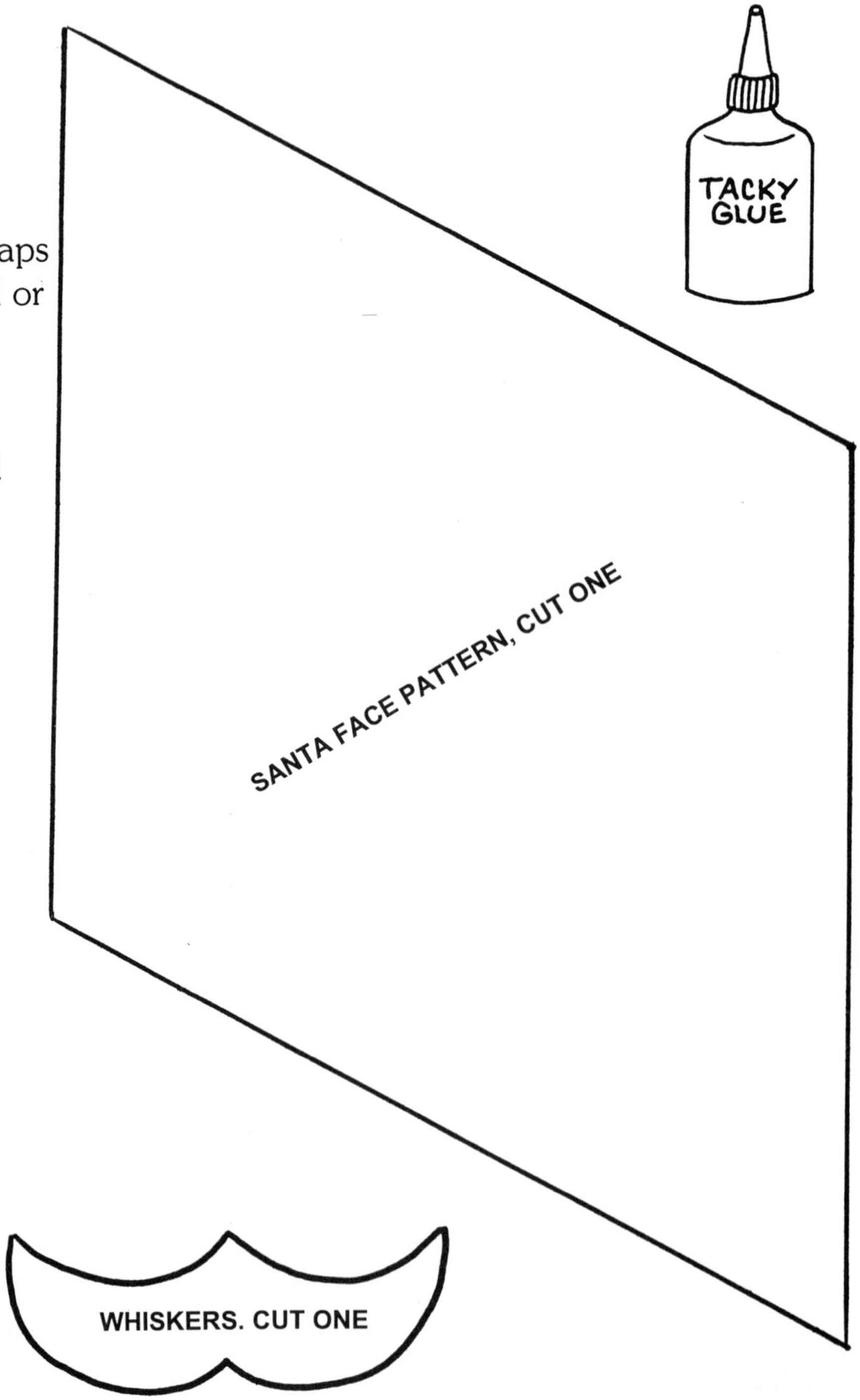

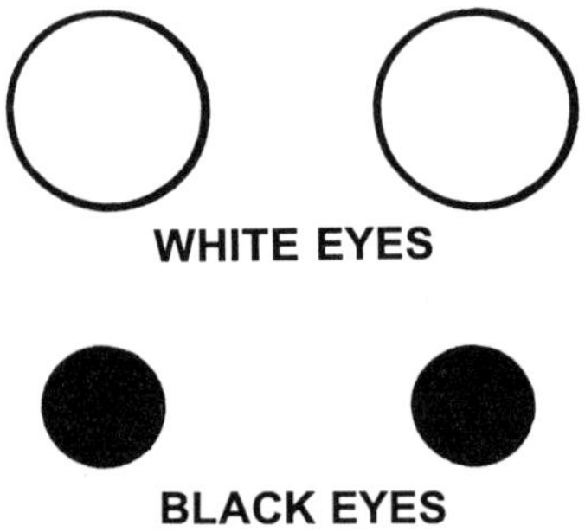

What to do:

1. Trace the patterns onto tracing paper and cut them out. Cut the Santa face out of red felt. Cut whiskers from white felt and eye parts from white and black felt.

2. Push chenille stem through jingle bell and pull stem ends even below the bell. Twist chenille stems together below the jingle bell and glue ends on the felt, as shown. The chenille stem will shape and stabilize the head.

3. Fold the face in half, chenille stem on the inside.

4. Use the needle and yarn to sew one edge closed from top to bottom. Use small stitches.

5. Fill the head with three tablespoons of rice. Sew the second edge closed.

6. Glue eyes and whiskers on the face.

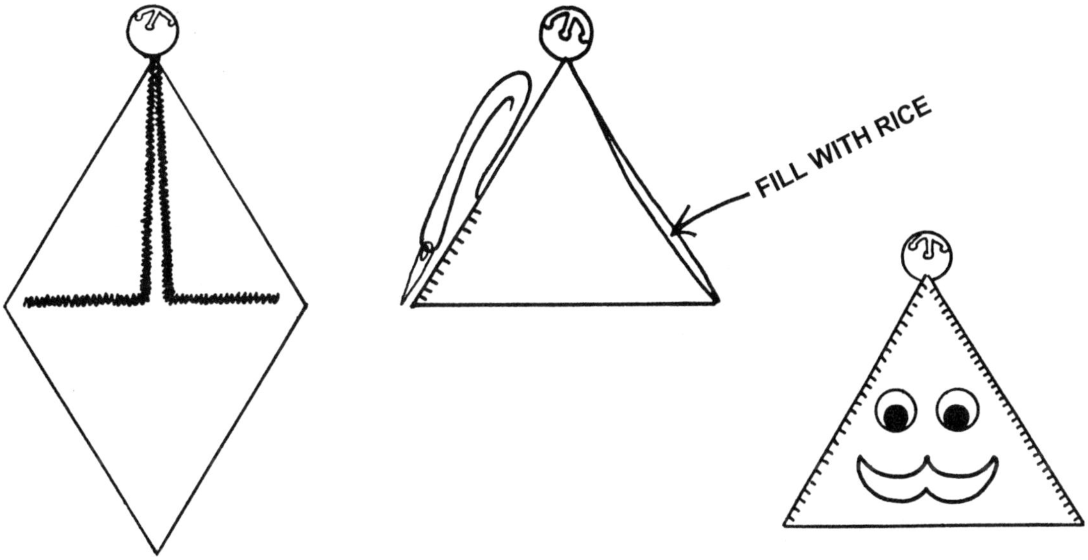

How to sew overhand stitch: Cut a piece of yarn about the length of your arm. Push one end through the needle's eye and knot the other end. Starting between the two felt layers so that the knot is hidden, push the needle to the front edge. Pull until all the yarn comes through. Bring the needle over the top edge to the back, then push it from back to front edge through both felt layers, near the previous stitch, and so on. Make small, even stitches. Do not pull the yarn too tightly. To finish off, sew two stitches over the top of the last one. Then push the needle a bit backward between the felt layers, along the edge, and cut the yarn.

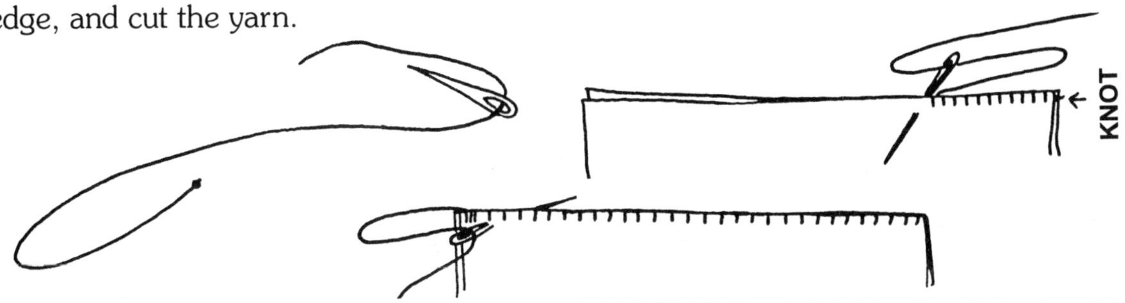

CHRISTMAS WATCHMAN

This little Santa's Elf announces visitors with jingle bells. It makes a nice keepsake gift to use for many Christmas seasons to come.

You will need:

- ❑ Small lid from dairy container, 3" (8 cm) wide
- ❑ Scissors
- ❑ Red yarn
- ❑ Wooden bead for body, natural color, 1 1/2" (38 mm)
- ❑ Wooden bead for head, natural color, 1" (25 mm)
- ❑ Wooden bead for arm, natural color, 1/2"(13 mm)
- ❑ Carpenter's glue
- ❑ Masking tape
- ❑ Red ribbon for bow
- ❑ Tracing paper and pen
- ❑ Red felt
- ❑ Tacky glue
- ❑ Black fine point permanent marker
- ❑ Three medium-sized jingle bells or liberty bells
- ❑ String

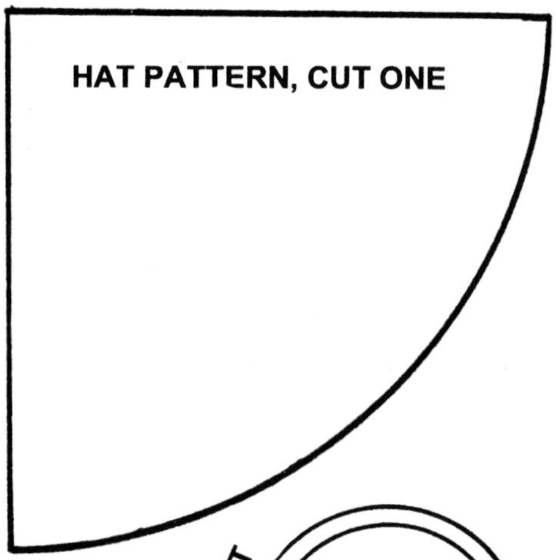

What to do:

1. Cut out the center from the dairy container lid, keeping only the rim. This makes a ring to fit over the doorknob. Wrap red yarn around the rim, covering it completely. Tie yarn ends together at lower end of ring and cut off.

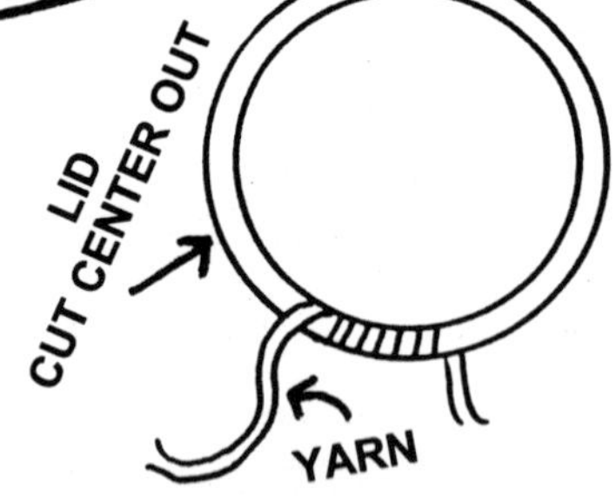

2. Make the elf: Using carpenter's glue, glue the head bead (holes on top and bottom) on the larger bead (holes sideways). Hold them together with masking tape until dry. Glue arm bead on one side of the body (holes on top and bottom), again holding them together with masking tape until dry. Remove the tape.

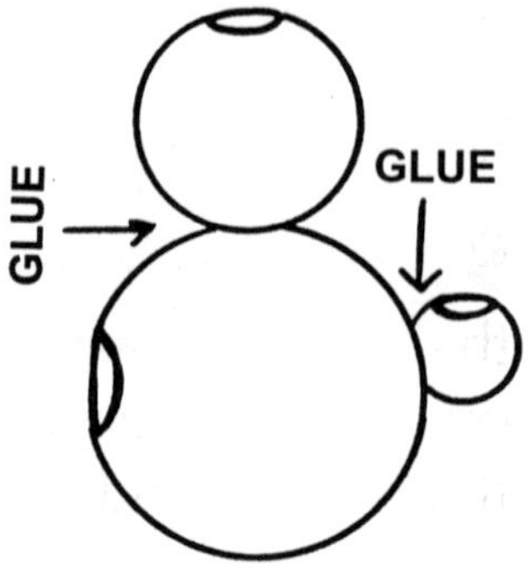

3. Take a piece of red yarn, about two yards (180 cm) long. Using the masking tape, attach one end securely to something solid (like a refrigerator). Hold the loose end securely and twist it to one side over and over until it is tightly twisted, then fold the yarn in half and it will twist around itself into a nice cord. Remove the masking tape. Tie one end to the lower end of the ring.

4. Wrap red ribbon around the lower end of the ring to cover the knots and tie the ribbon ends into a bow.

5. Push lower end of the hanging red cord through the "arm" bead. Make a knot below the arm about 7" (18 cm) beneath the ring.

6. Trace the hat pattern and mitten-scarf pattern onto tracing paper and cut them out. Trace the patterns on red felt and cut them out.

7. Spread a strip of tacky glue along one back edge of the hat. Overlap the back edges and glue them together to make a cone hat. Spread a strip of tacky glue around the elf's head and glue the hat on. Glue the scarf around the neck so that the mitten end will cover the hole at the body's side. Glue the top edge of the hat to the yarn cord with tacky glue.

8. Using the marker, draw a face.

9. With the string, tie three jingle bells to the hanging yarn cord, one on the hat top, one at the bottom, and one halfway between the bottom and the elf.

BLUE ANGEL CUTIE

This adorable, tiny angel becomes one of the precious keepsake Christmas ornaments. Write your name and year underneath the cork to remind people who made it and when.

You will need:

- ❑ Cork (from wine bottle)
- ❑ Scissors
- ❑ Glue stick
- ❑ Blue foil
- ❑ Wooden bead, natural color, 1" (25 mm)
- ❑ Yellow curling ribbon
- ❑ Tacky glue
- ❑ Tracing paper and pencil
- ❑ Construction paper
- ❑ Double-sided tape
- ❑ Tinsel stem, 6" (15 cm) long (metallic pipe cleaner)
- ❑ Black fine point permanent marker

What to do:

1. Hollow out the cork top with the tip of the scissors about 1/4" (6 mm) deep, as shown with the broken line in the illustration.

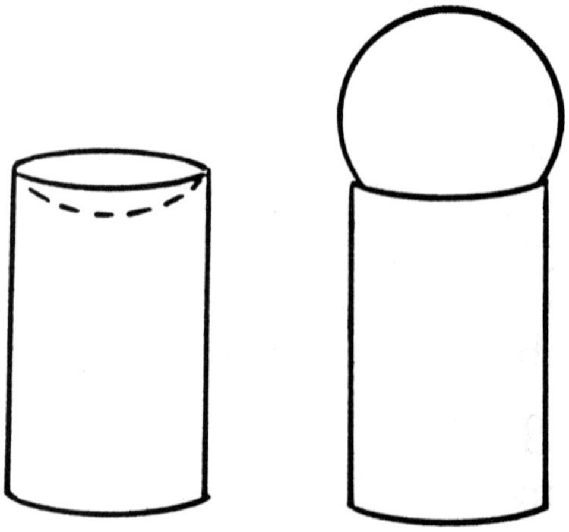

2. Cut a piece of blue foil to fit all around the cork and glue it in place with the glue stick.

3. Glue the head into the cork top hole with the tacky glue.

4. Curl a piece of yellow ribbon by pulling it against the blade of the scissors. Then split it apart into several tiny strands. Put tacky glue onto the head top and press the curly ribbon hair into the glue.

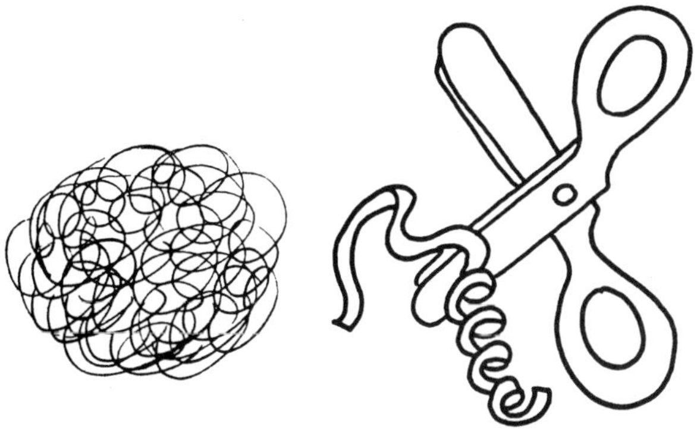

5. Glue blue foil on each side of a 5" (13 cm) square of construction paper with the glue stick. Trace the wings onto tracing paper and cut them out. Then trace them on the foil-covered construction paper and cut out.

6. Curve the wing tips gently toward the front around the length of the pencil. Attach the wings at the back of the cork body with the double-sided tape.

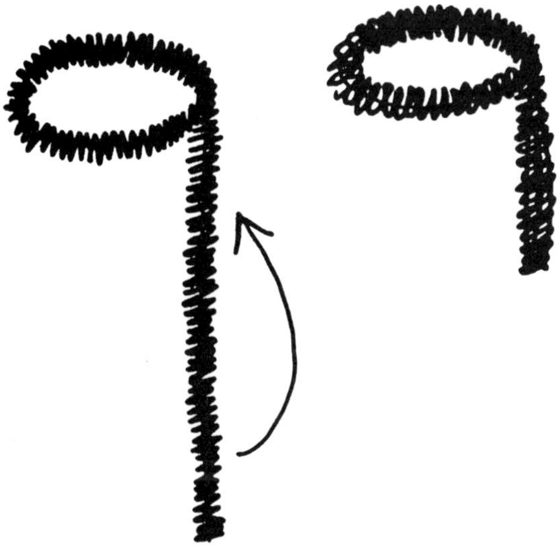

7. Twist one end of the tinsel stem into a tiny halo. Fold and twist the remaining end into a stiff stick. Dip the lower end of the halo stick into tacky glue and push it firmly into the center hole of the head through the hair.

8. Draw the eyes and mouth.

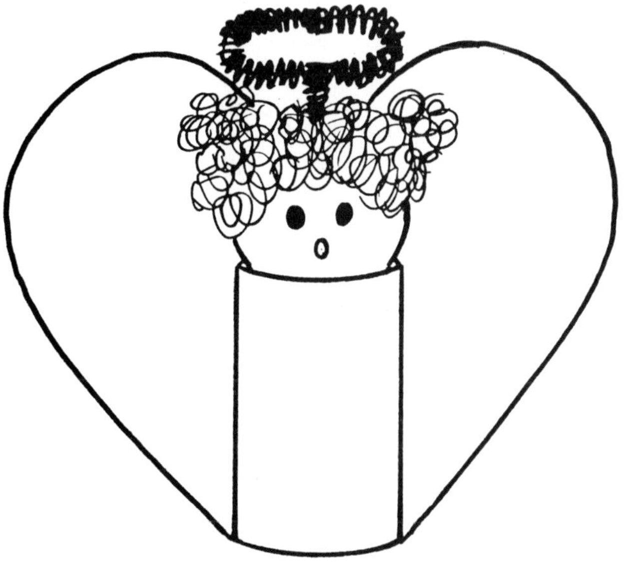

APPLE TWINS

This is one of the easiest ideas in this book. Turn simple felt and a chenille stem magically into an attractive Christmas ornament to hang on the tree or over a doorknob.

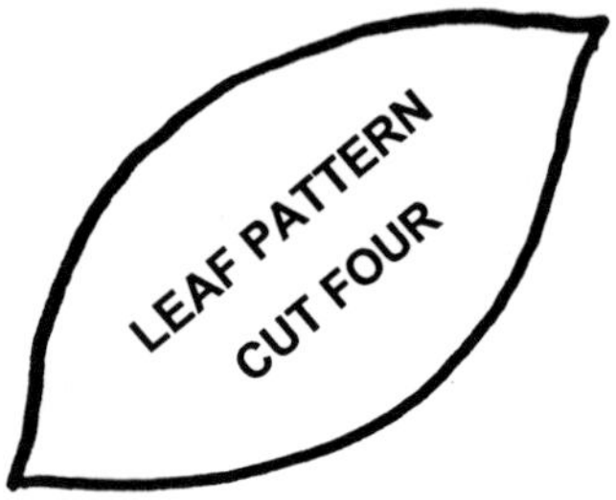

You will need:

- ❑ Tracing paper and pen
- ❑ Scissors
- ❑ Red felt
- ❑ Green felt
- ❑ Black chenille stem
- ❑ Tacky glue

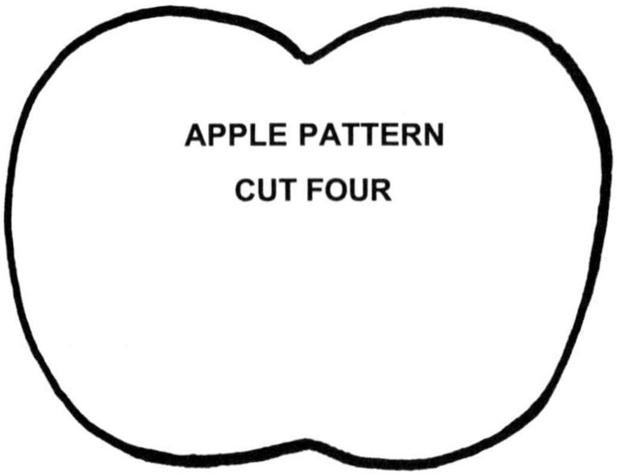

What to do:

1. Trace the pattern pieces onto tracing paper and cut them out.

2. Cut four apples from red felt and four leaves from green felt.

3. Turn the chenille stem into a hook and glue it between two apples with the ends showing a bit below the apples, as shown. (Chenille stem makes a hanger for the Christmas tree or the doorknob.)

4. Glue two leaves at the top of each apple, as shown.

5. Glue the second set of felt apples on top of the first ones.

RAFFIA WREATH

Florists sell natural raffia strands for pennies. Nature yields tiny alder or tamarack cones. Tie them together into a charmingly simple mini-wreath for your Christmas tree.

You will need:

- ❑ Raffia
- ❑ Scissors
- ❑ Two tiny alder or tamarack cones

What to do:

1. Hold a long strand of raffia between your outstretched hands. Twist one end over and over to one side. Then fold the raffia strand in half so it will twist around itself into a nice cord.

2. Form the twisted raffia cord into a small circle. Trim ends, as shown.

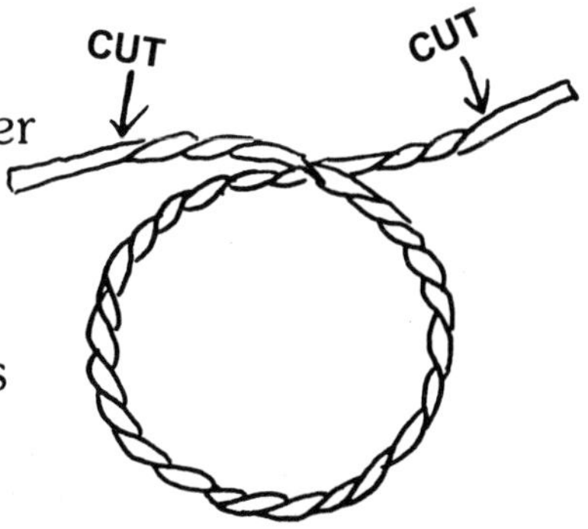

3. Tie a strand of raffia around center top to keep the wreath closed.

4. Tear off another thin strand of raffia. Wind one end around the cones and slide the raffia under the cone layers at top. (If the cones are tightly closed, they will open their layers in warm room or oven.) Use the rest of the raffia strand to tie the cones to the wreath top and tie the raffia ends into a loop for hanging.

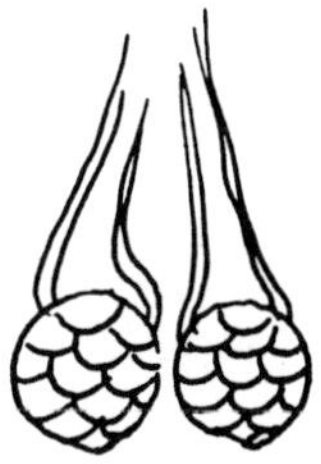

5. Tie another thin strand of raffia at the top of the wreath into a bow.

DOORKNOB GIFTS

Doorknobs become festive at Christmas time! You can decorate the "gift boxes" with foil stars, glitter, felt cutouts, tiny gift tags, etc., or use pretty gift paper scraps instead of felt for the "boxes" (using stiff cardboard between the two paper layers). This gift row also makes a lovely tree ornament.

You will need:

- ❑ Small yogurt container, 3" (8 cm) wide
- ❑ Scissors
- ❑ Green yarn
- ❑ One yard (90 cm) of green ribbon, 1/4" (6 mm) wide
- ❑ Two small jingle bells or liberty bells
- ❑ Red felt
- ❑ Stiff cardboard
- ❑ Glue stick
- ❑ Red and white curling ribbon

What to do:

1. Cut a 1/2" (13 mm) wide ring from the top edge of a small yogurt container. This will fit over the doorknob.

2. Wrap green yarn around the ring, covering it completely. Tie the yarn ends together at the bottom and cut the ends off.

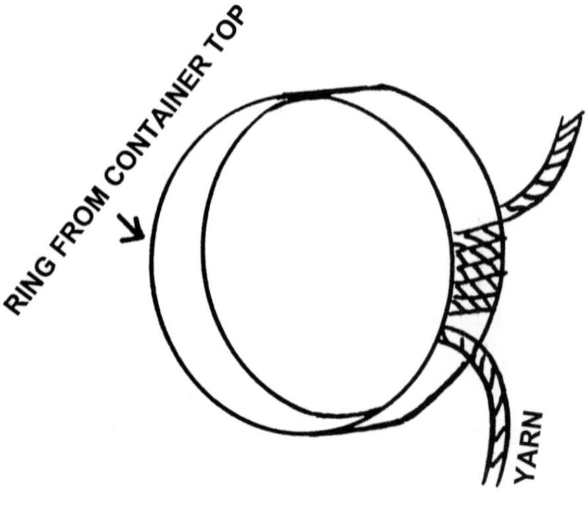

3. Cut a 20” (50 cm) long piece from the green ribbon and tie one end to the bottom of the ring.

4. Wrap the remaining piece of green ribbon around the knots and tie it into a bow.

5. Push the lower end of the ribbon through two jingle bells. Knot the ribbon at the lower end and between the bells.

6. Gift boxes: Cut six rectangles of red felt and three rectangles of stiff cardboard, about 3" x 2" (8 cm x 5 cm) each. Run the glue stick over one side of each cardboard piece and glue them onto three of the felt rectangles. Place them on the table, as shown, cardboard side up. Run the glue stick over the top of the cardboard pieces, glue the green ribbon on center top and then the remaining three felt pieces on top.

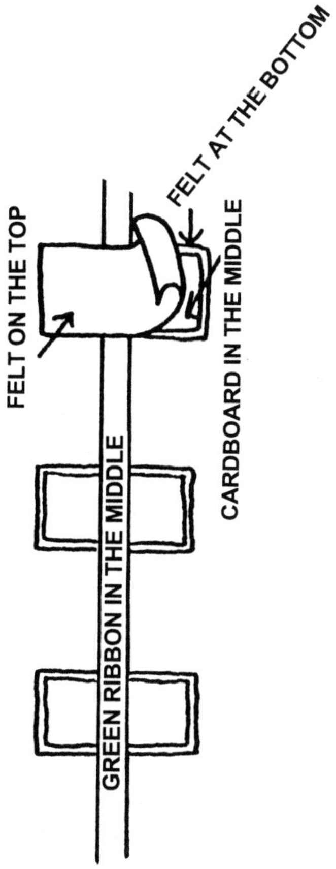

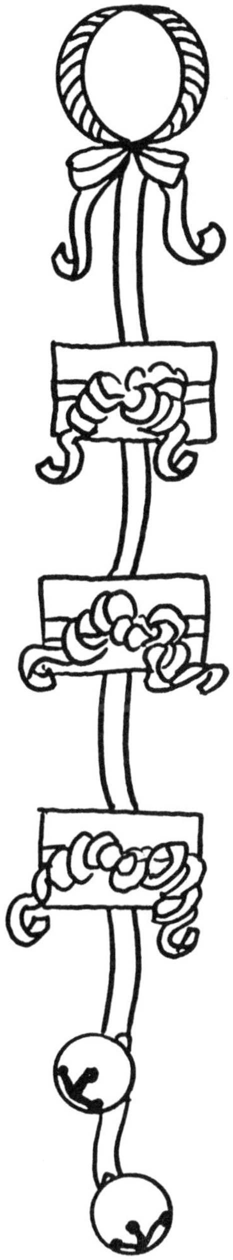

7. Wrap each of the three gift boxes with curling ribbon. Curl ribbon ends with the blade of the scissors.

GLITTERING ANGEL

You'll be amazed to see how a simple sheet of paper becomes a wonderful angel. This is nice on a tabletop, window sill or bookshelf.

You will need:

- ❑ Sheet of stiff white paper, legal size 8 1/2" x 14" (22 cm x 36 cm)
- ❑ Scissors
- ❑ White liquid glue
- ❑ Gold glitter
- ❑ Waxed paper
- ❑ Piece of string
- ❑ Double-sided tape
- ❑ Angel face sticker
- ❑ Large plastic cap from a spray can

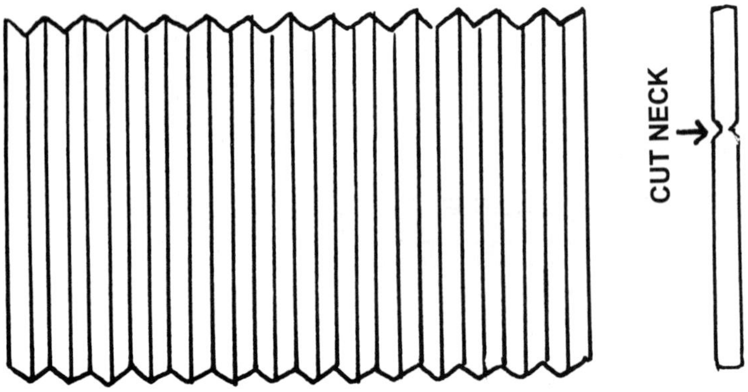

What to do:

1. Starting at one short end, pleat the entire paper in 1/2" (13 mm) folds, accordion style.

2. Press the pleats tightly together. Cut through all the layers to make the neck, as shown. (Be careful not to cut all the way through.)

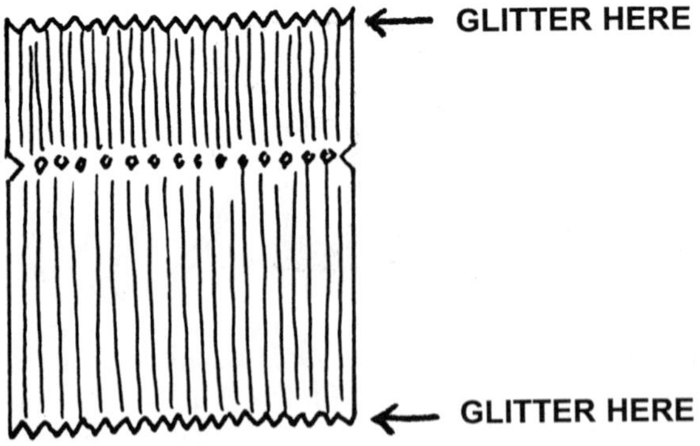

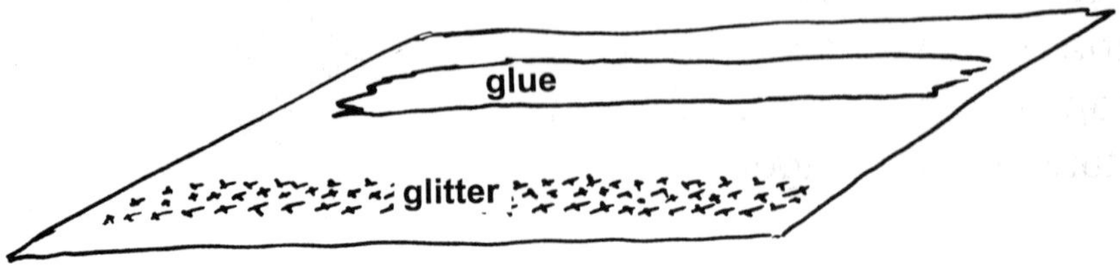

3. Spread the paper slightly to open the pleats out a bit (but keep the accordion shape). Pour a thick line of glue onto the waxed paper and a thick line of glitter near the glue line. Dip top and bottom accordion edges first into the glue, then into the glitter. Let dry on a clean sheet of waxed paper. The glue will be transparent after it dries and the glitter will make a stiff beautiful edge at the wing and skirt ends.

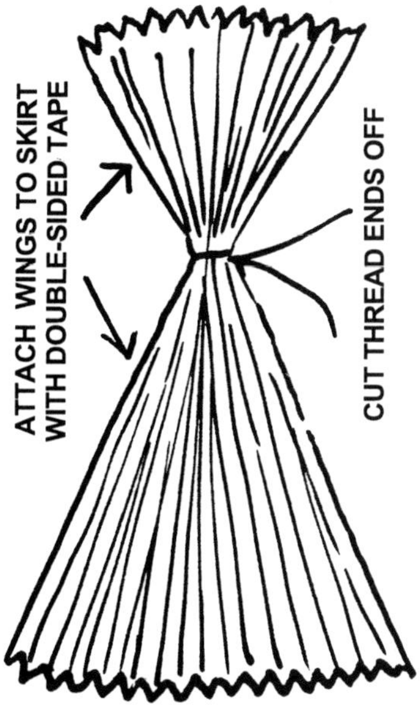

4. Tie a piece of string around the neck. Cut the string ends off.

5. Gently open the pleats. Use double-sided tape to attach the wing edges to skirt edges at each side.

6. Glue the angel sticker on the face using white liquid glue.

7. Using double-sided tape, at back, attach the plastic cap to skirt hem line, lower edges even. The cap makes a sturdy tabletop stand for the angel.

CHRISTMAS GNOME CUTIE

Everyone loves little gnomes at Christmas! Make lots of these so you have extras to give to all your friends and relatives. Write your name and year underneath the cork.

You will need:

- ❑ Cork (from wine bottle)
- ❑ Scissors
- ❑ Red felt
- ❑ Grey felt scrap
- ❑ Wooden bead, natural color, 1" (25 mm)
- ❑ Tacky glue
- ❑ Tracing paper and pen
- ❑ Black fine point permanent marker
- ❑ Red chenille stem
- ❑ Medium-sized liberty bell or jingle bell

What to do:

1. Hollow out the cork top with the tip of the scissors 1/4" (6 mm) deep, as shown with broken line in the illustration.

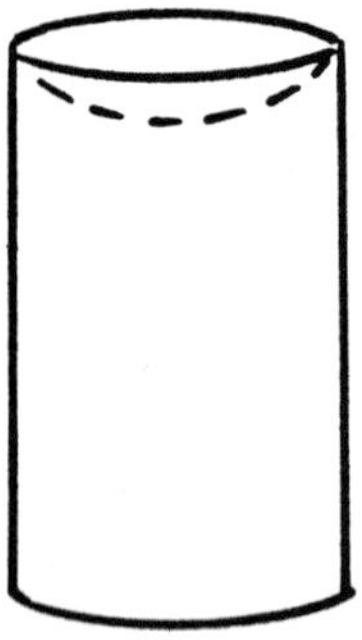

2. Cut a piece of red felt to fit around the cork and glue it in place.

3. Beard: Cut the lower edge of a tiny strip of grey felt into fringes, as shown. Glue upper edge of the felt strip on the "chin" of the head bead.

4. Hat: Trace the hat pattern onto tracing paper and cut it out. Trace the pattern onto red felt and cut it out. Spread a strip of tacky glue along one back edge of the hat. Overlap back edges and glue them together to make a cone hat. Spread a strip of tacky glue around the gnome's head and glue the hat on.

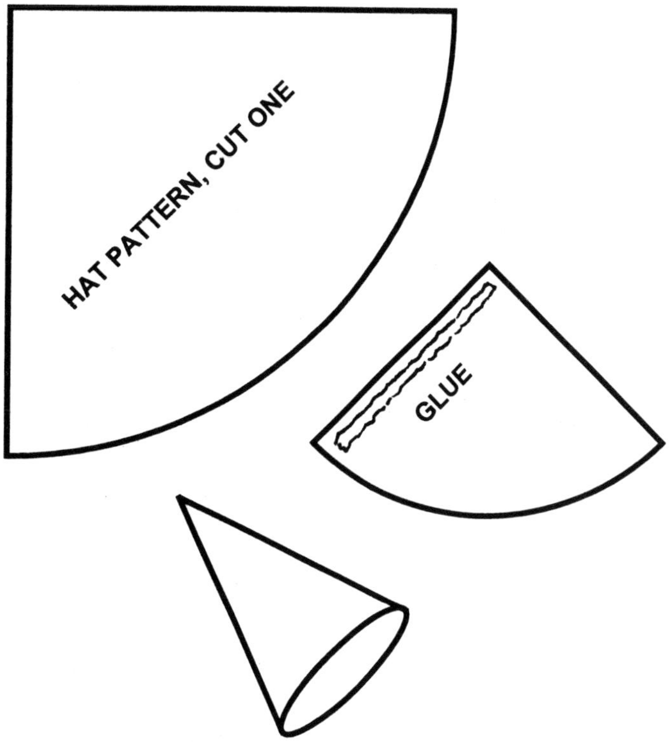

5. Using the marker, draw the eyes and the mouth.

6. Put tacky glue into the cork top hole, press the center of the chenille stem into it, add more tacky glue and then press the head on top of the chenille stem. Hold the head down tightly for several seconds so that the glue will hold. Let dry thoroughly.

7. Push one end of the chenille stem arm through the bell, bring the ends around to the front and twist them together to make hands holding the bell. Cut off the chenille stem ends.

SLEEPY ANGEL

Don't throw away the foil inner seals from dairy containers! Look what charming little angels they make! These are lovely hanging in windows.

You will need:

- ❑ Two aluminum foil inner seals from dairy containers (or foil and construction paper)
- ❑ Glue stick
- ❑ Tracing paper and pencil
- ❑ Scissors
- ❑ Light-colored construction paper for face
- ❑ Black pen or fine point marker
- ❑ 10" (25 cm) of string

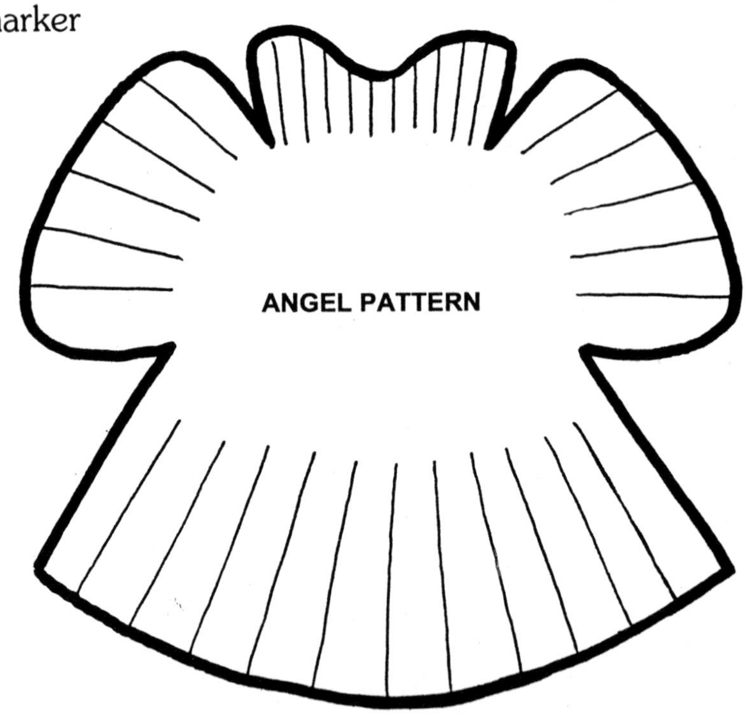

What to do:

1. Glue the foil seals together (printed side in) with a glue stick. (Or glue a sheet of construction paper between two sheets of aluminum foil.)

2. Trace the pattern onto tracing paper but do not cut it out. Put it on top of the double-layered foil seals (or foil-covered construction paper) and redraw the lines, pressing them onto the foil. Cut the angel out of the foil.

3. Cut a small circle from light-colored construction paper for the face. Draw the eyes and mouth with the black pen or marker. Glue the face in place.

4. Cut the skirt and wings into fringes and curl them up a bit around a pencil. Cut the hair into tiny strips, curve the strips frontward and then bring them down over the forehead to make bangs.

5. Knot the string ends together. Punch a tiny hole on top of the forehead (with a pencil tip), and push the string's loop end through, from front to back, to make a hanger. The hair will hide the knot.

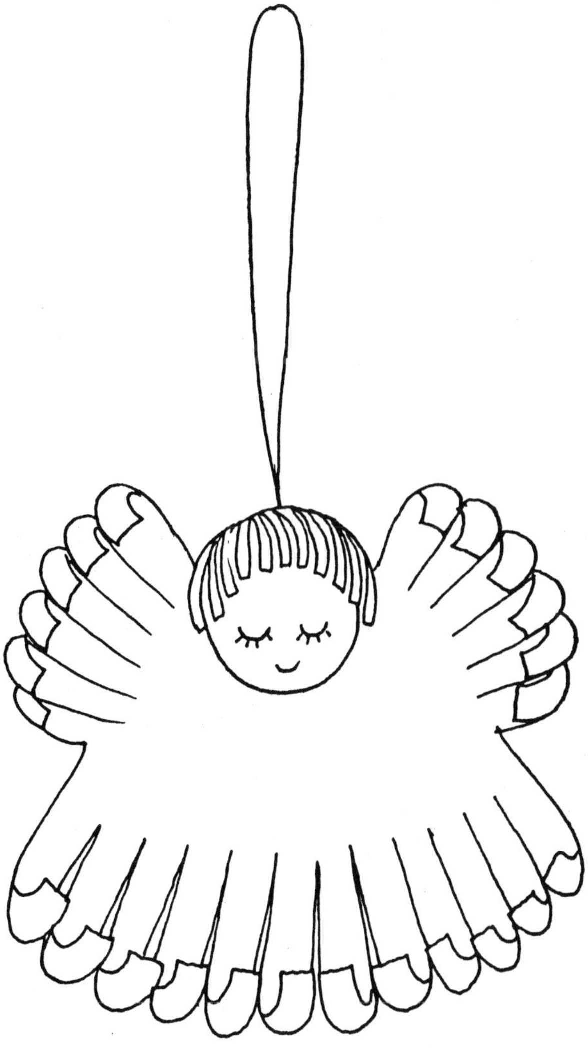

ROBIN REDBREAST

The practical snap-on frame is made from an empty dairy container. A robin makes a simple and beautiful design in the frame. Other possibilities using felt or bright paper scraps: flowers, trees, colorful fish...

You will need:

- ❑ Medium-sized dairy container with lid (from cottage cheese, yogurt or sour cream)
- ❑ Scissors
- ❑ 15" (38 cm) of string (dental floss works well)
- ❑ Transparent plastic bag (or a sheet of plastic wrap folded in half)
- ❑ Tracing paper and pen
- ❑ Red and black felt
- ❑ Glue stick or tacky glue

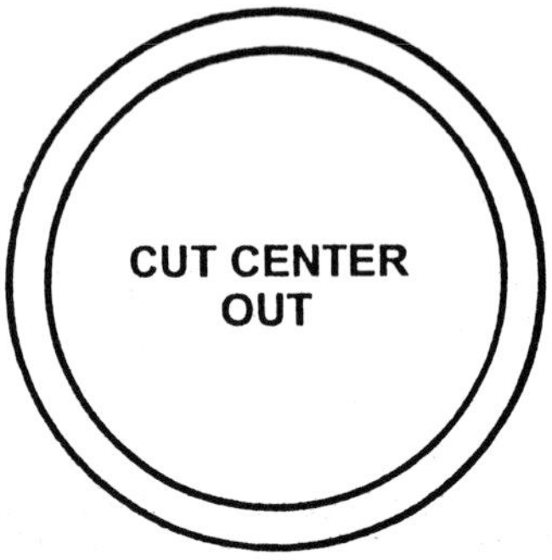

What to do:

1. Make a frame from the dairy container by cutting out the lid's center, keeping only the rim. Then cut off the lower part of the container, keeping only the rim.

2. Tie a piece of string around the lid rim to make a loop for hanging.

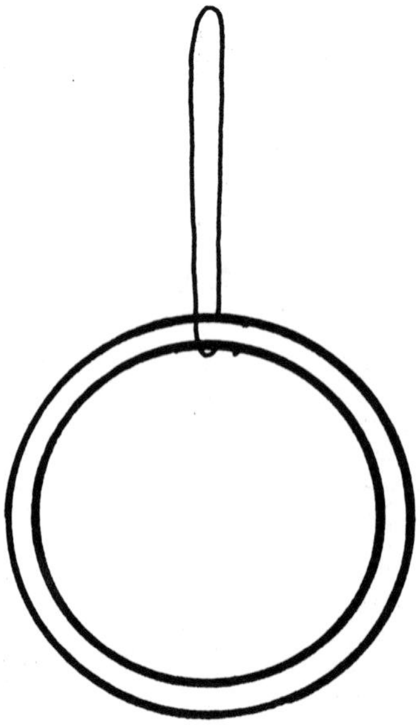

3. Lay the plastic bag between the two rims and snap them together so that the bag will be straight and tight. Cut off the extra plastic all around the outside of frame. Be careful not to cut the string!

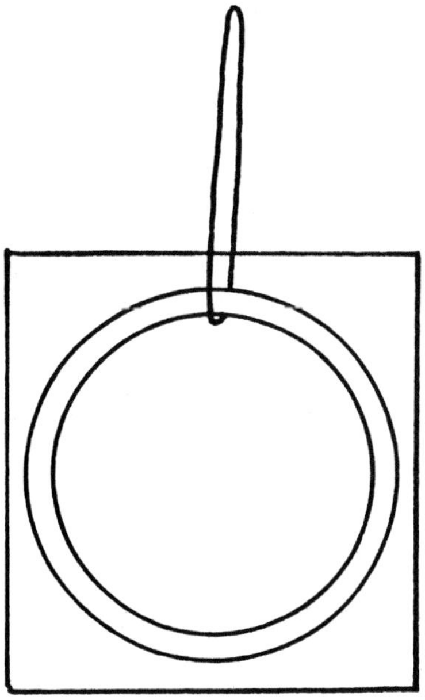

4. Trace the pattern pieces onto the tracing paper and cut them out.

5. Cut the upper part (wing/head) from black felt and the body from red felt.

6. Glue the robin in the middle of the plastic. Hang it in the window.

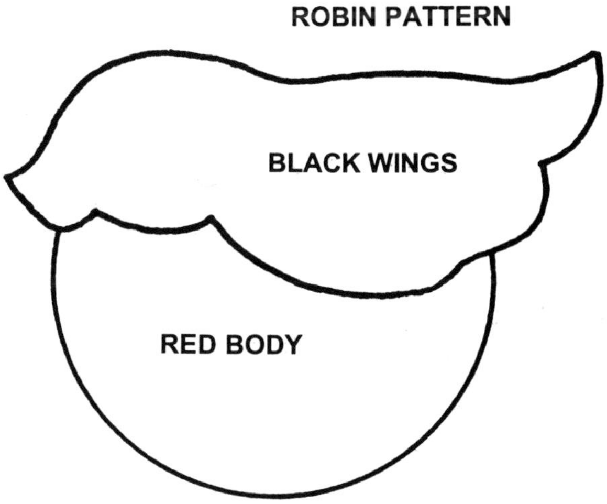

SCANDINAVIAN SPICE WREATH

All-purpose white liquid glue is so fabulous! It holds the allspice berries neatly together to make this simple tiny wreath. (Allspice berries cost only pennies when you buy them in bulk.) This wreath not only smells lovely but the dry berries rattle nicely. You can hang it on the Christmas tree or in the kitchen.

You will need:

- ❑ Tracing paper and pencil
- ❑ Heavy duty aluminum foil
- ❑ White liquid glue
- ❑ Allspice (whole berries), about 1/4 cup (50 ml)
- ❑ 10" (25 cm) of string
- ❑ 15" (38 cm) of narrow red ribbon

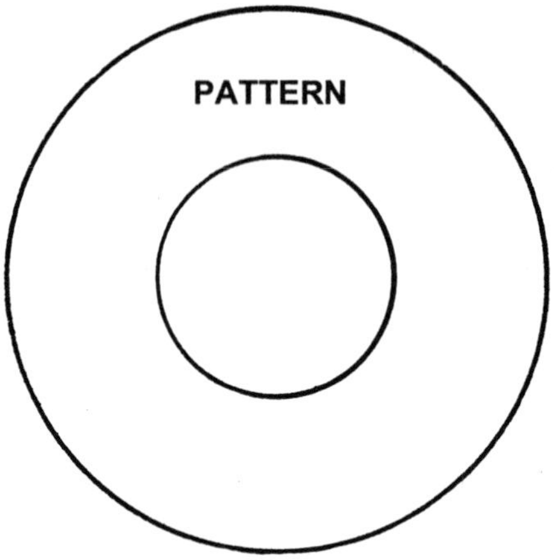

What to do:

1. Trace the "donut" pattern onto tracing paper but do not cut it out. Put the tracing paper on top of the aluminum foil and trace the lines to press them into the foil, but do not cut the foil. (The foil is used just as a working surface so the wreath will peel off easily from it later.) Remove the tracing paper but save it as a pattern if you want to make another wreath.

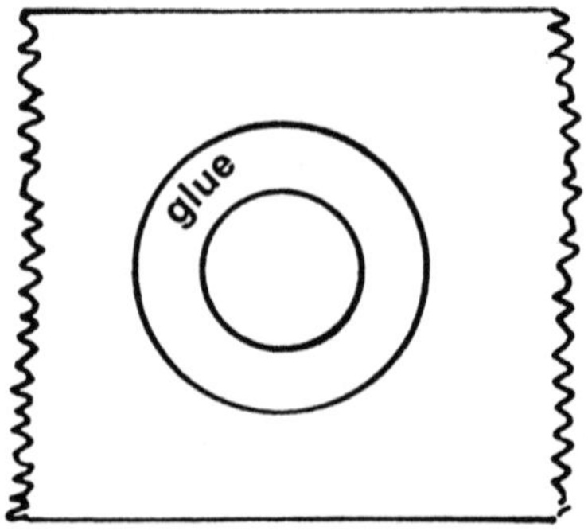

2. Spread a generous layer of liquid glue right on the foil. Cover the "donut" area completely.

3. Drop allspice berries into the glue, side by side, until all of the glue is covered. Let it dry thoroughly overnight.

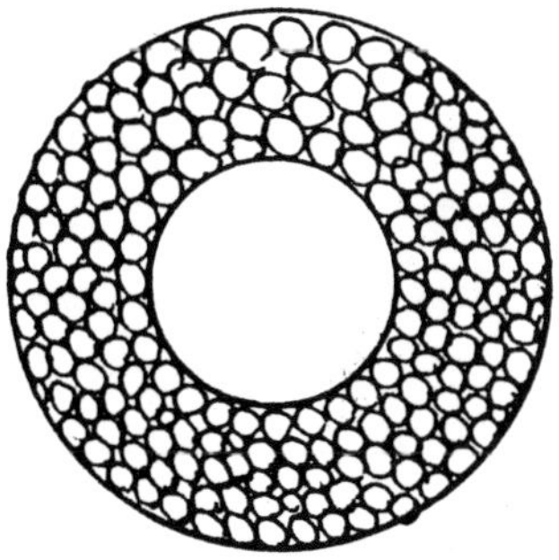

4. When the glue has dried into a shiny, transparent layer, peel the wreath off and turn it upside down on the foil. Spread more glue generously on the back of the wreath and drop allspice berries in the glue, again until covered. Let dry very well overnight. The glue will become invisible and the wreath will be loose on the foil. Discard the foil.

5. Tie the string around the top to make a loop. Tie the ribbon into a bow on the top.

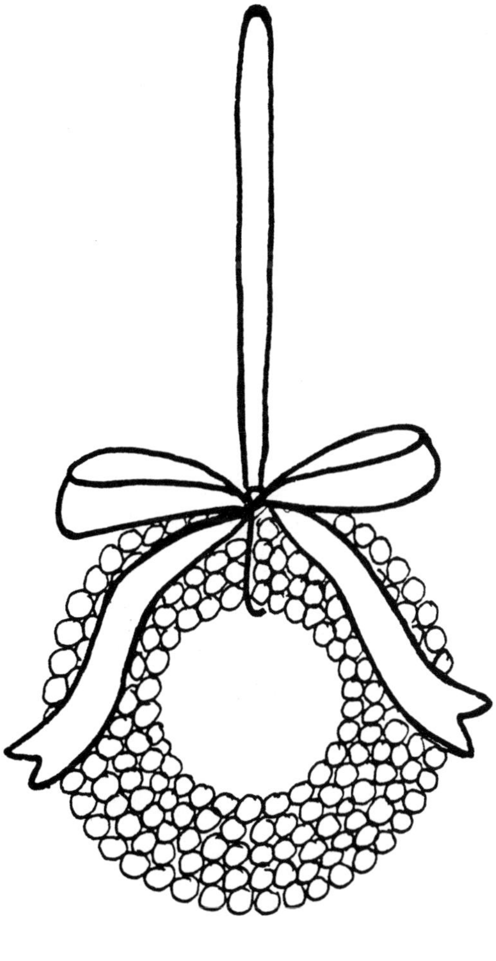

SILVER REINDEER

This makes a beautiful tabletop decoration at Christmas time. A row of reindeer makes a stunning centerpiece. (A piece of double-sided tape underneath keeps it upright on the tabletop.)

You will need:

- ❑ Tracing paper and pencil
- ❑ Scissors
- ❑ Thin cardboard
- ❑ Self-adhesive silver metallic paper (or foil and glue stick)
- ❑ Double-sided tape

What to do:

1. Trace the reindeer and antlers onto tracing paper and cut them out.

2. Stick self-adhesive metallic paper onto thin cardboard (or glue foil onto cardboard), large enough for the patterns. Trace the reindeer and antlers onto the cardboard. Cut them out. Carefully cut out the squares between the legs. (Start by pushing the blade of the scissors through the center of the square and cutting a slit into each of the four corners, then cut all around and discard the pieces.)

3. Fold the reindeer where shown. Stick the top edges together at the tabs with double-sided tape.

4. Fold the antlers in half, metallic side out. Attach them behind the ears (between the two layers) using the double-sided tape.

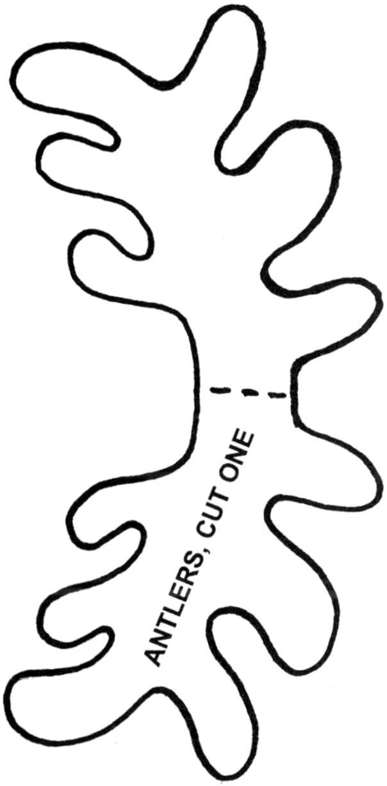
ANTLERS, CUT ONE

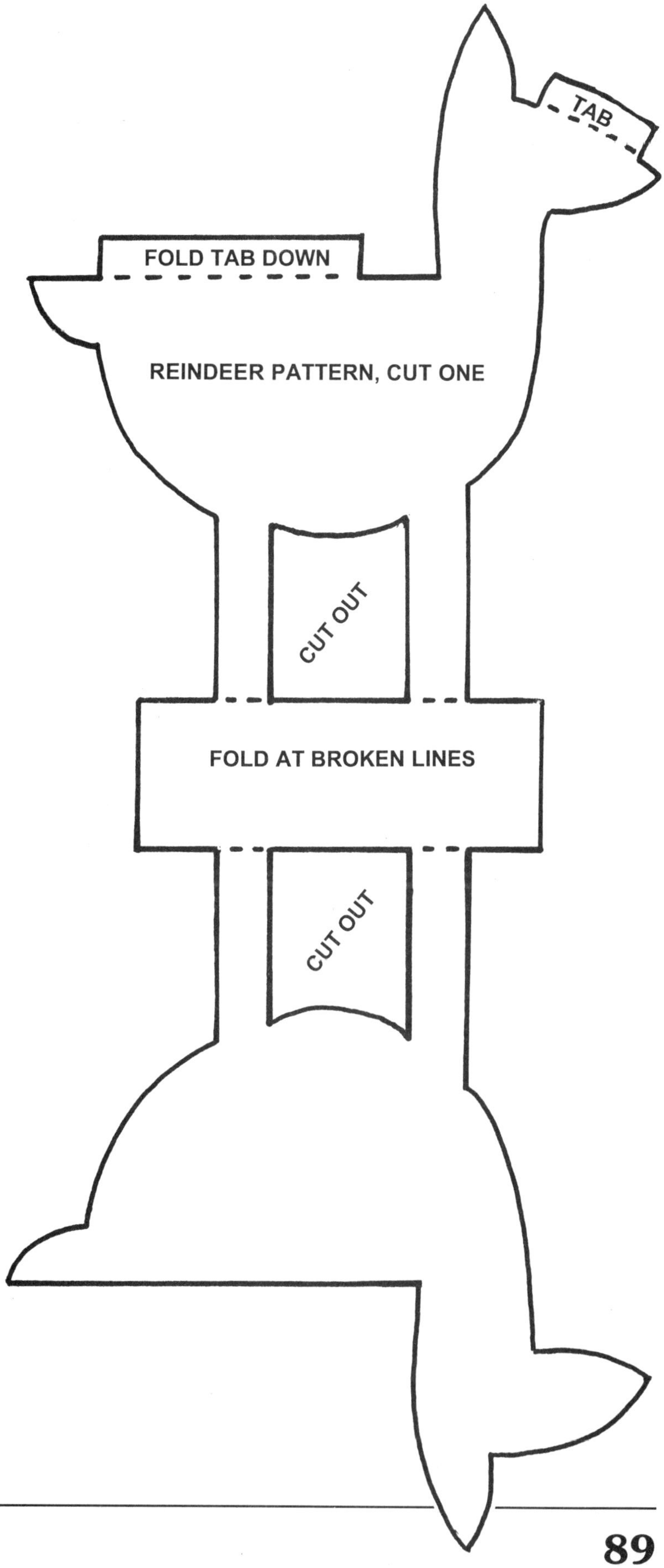
TAB
FOLD TAB DOWN
REINDEER PATTERN, CUT ONE
CUT OUT
FOLD AT BROKEN LINES
CUT OUT

SANTA'S LITTLE HELPER

Wooden beads and felt make great little Santa's Helpers for the Christmas tree or dinner table.

You will need:

- ❑ Wooden bead, natural color, 1" (25 mm)
- ❑ Wooden bead, natural color, 1 1/2" (38 mm)
- ❑ Carpenter's glue
- ❑ Masking tape
- ❑ Tracing paper and pen
- ❑ Scissors
- ❑ Red felt
- ❑ Tacky glue
- ❑ Black fine point permanent marker
- ❑ Optional: Yarn or metallic tinsel stem for hanging

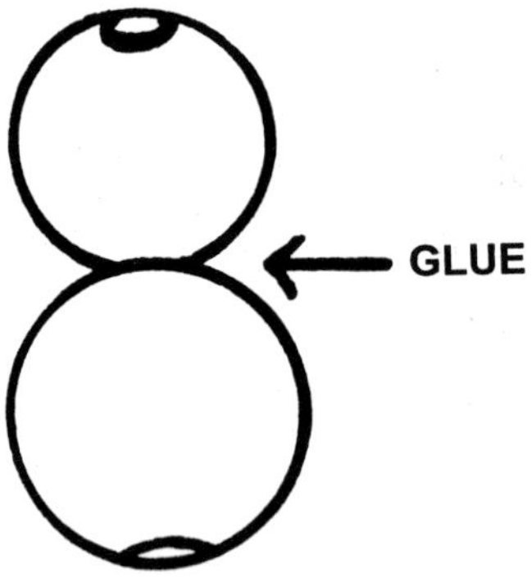

What to do:

1. With carpenter's glue, glue the smaller bead onto the larger one. Match up the holes so that they are at the top and bottom. Wrap a piece of masking tape around the beads to hold them in place until the glue is dry. Remove the tape.

2. Trace the hat pattern onto tracing paper and cut it out. Trace the pattern onto red felt and cut it out.

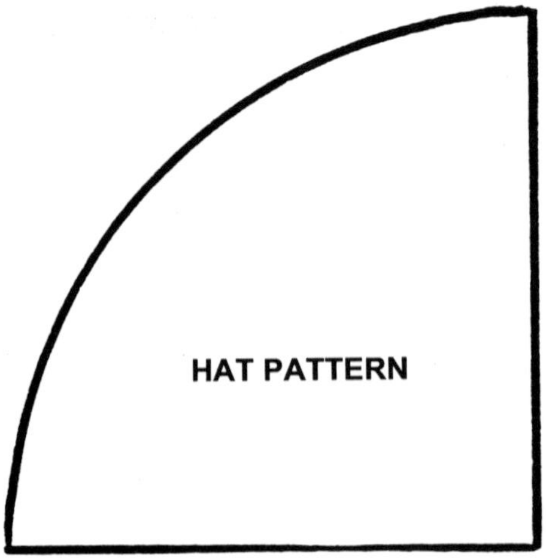

3. Spread a strip of tacky glue along one back edge of the hat. Overlap the back edges and glue them together to make a cone hat.

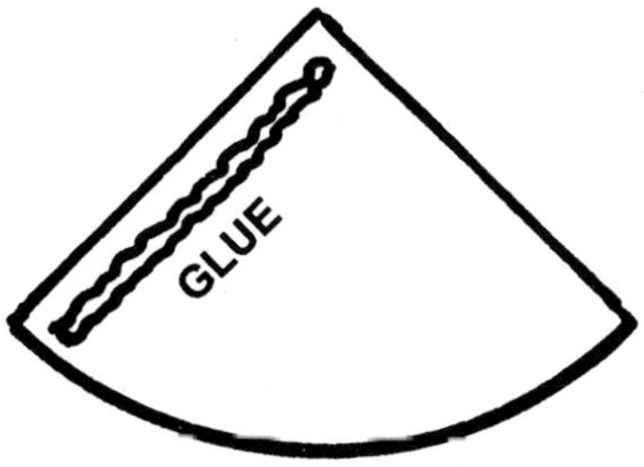

4. Spread a strip of tacky glue around the bead head and glue the hat on.

5. Using the marker, draw the eyes and mouth.

6. If you want to hang this Santa's Helper on the tree, make a long loop from thick twisted yarn or tinsel stem and pull it through the holes before you glue the hat on. (Use a chenille stem or florist wire as a hook to pull the yarn through the holes.) Make a knot at the bottom and push the knot to the inside, out of sight. Add a dab of glue so that the knot will stay in place. Cut a tiny circle of red felt and glue it over the bottom hole.

FREDDIE THE SNOWMAN

Wooden beads and felt make this adorable snowman for your Christmas tree. The top hat hides a little secret underneath; it is a bottle cap covered with felt.

You will need:

- ❑ Wooden bead, natural color, 1" (25 mm)
- ❑ Wooden bead, natural color, 1 1/2" (38 mm)
- ❑ Carpenter's glue
- ❑ Masking tape
- ❑ Bottle cap (from small cosmetic or food bottle)
- ❑ Black and red felt scraps
- ❑ Scissors
- ❑ Tacky glue
- ❑ Black fine point permanent marker
- ❑ 20" (50 cm) of long red cord (or yarn twisted into thick cord)

What to do:

1. With carpenter's glue, glue the smaller bead (holes sideways) onto the larger one (holes on top and bottom). Wrap a piece of masking tape around the beads to hold them in place until the glue is dry. Remove the tape.

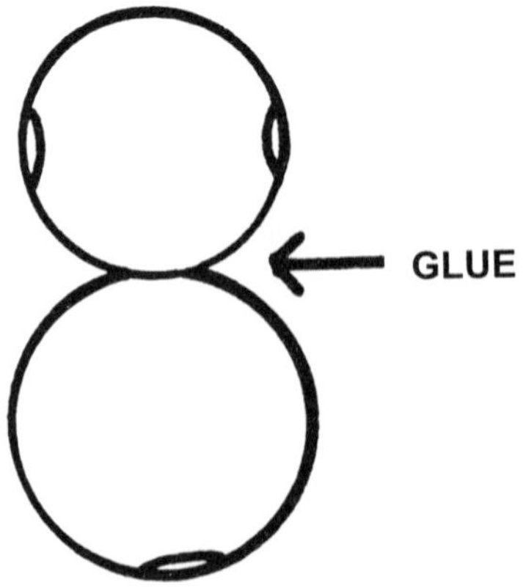

2. Make a top hat using the bottle cap and black felt. Glue a felt circle on the cap top and a felt strip around the sides. Cut another felt circle a bit larger than the cap bottom and glue it on top of the head. Glue the top hat on the felt circle.

3. Using the marker, draw the eyes, mouth and buttons.

4. Cut the scarf from red felt. Cut the ends into fringes. Dab tacky glue in the center and tie the scarf around the neck, gluing it in place.

5. Thread cord through the "ear holes" to hang the snowman on the tree.

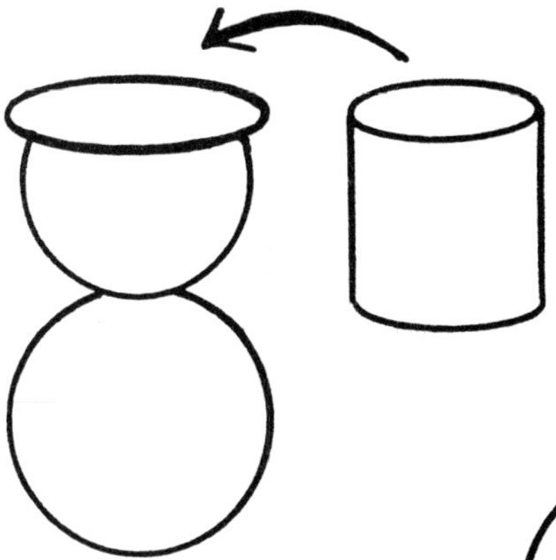

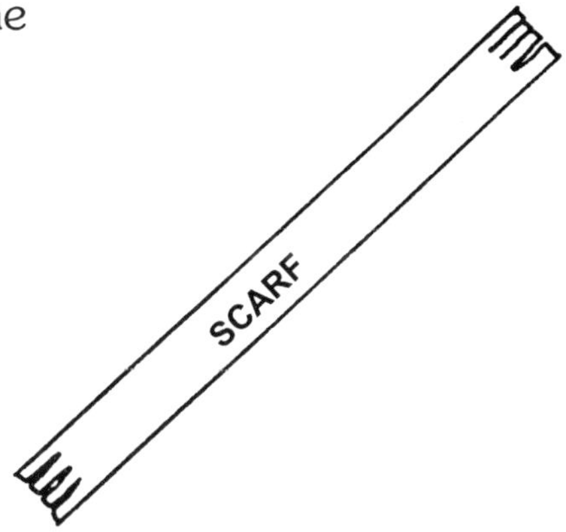

CHRISTMAS TREE BAUBLE

Rescue small lids from the trash! They make great little frames for photo ornaments.

You will need:

- ❑ Small lid from jar or bottle, about 1 1/2" (4 cm) wide
- ❑ Aluminum foil (aluminum inner seals from dairy containers are perfect!)
- ❑ Scissors
- ❑ Glue stick
- ❑ Two pieces of curling ribbon, 10" and 24" (25 cm and 61 cm) long
- ❑ Photo, sticker or magazine cutout (same size as the lid)

What to do:

1. Cut a piece of foil a little bigger than your lid. Wrap the foil on the outside of the lid and press the edges tightly over the rim toward the inside.

2. Take the longer piece of ribbon. Starting 4" (10 cm) from one end, glue it around the outside of the rim, knot the ends together at top, then fold the longer end into a loop and tie it together with the shorter end.

3. Tie the shorter piece of ribbon around the lower end of the loop into a bow. Curl loose ribbon ends by pulling them gently against the blade of the scissors.

4. Glue a photo, sticker or magazine picture inside.

CANDLE STAND

A simple tuna can makes a great candle holder as it happens to be just the right size for a fat candle. Decorate it with foil, pine cones and ribbons.

You will need:

- ❑ Empty tuna can, large size
- ❑ Aluminum foil
- ❑ Scissors
- ❑ Two 20" (50 cm) pieces of narrow curling ribbon, one red and one green
- ❑ Two small pine cones
- ❑ Dental floss or strong thread
- ❑ Fat red or green candle
- ❑ Optional: Glitter and glue stick

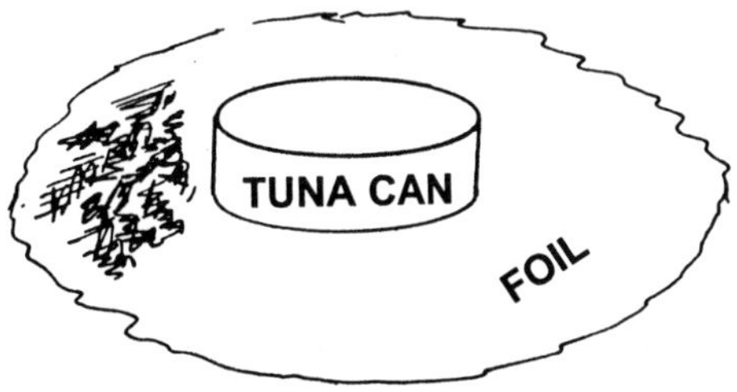

What to do:

1. Remove the label and wash and dry the tuna can thoroughly.

2. Crinkle a sheet of aluminum foil (for strength and texture), then straighten it and wrap it around the bottom and sides of the can, tucking the ends tightly inside the can.

3. Wrap ribbons around the can and tie the ends together into a bow. Curl the ends by pulling them gently against the blade of the scissors.

4. Slip a piece of dental floss between the ribbons and the can. Tie pine cones on each side of the bow. (The dental floss slides under the cone layers at the top so that you can tie them to the ribbons.)

5. If desired, rub a glue stick around the middle of the candle and sprinkle on some glitter for a festive touch.

LOVE ROW TREE ORNAMENT

This simple row of red felt hearts will look so Christmasy on any tree. Think of other simple designs such as pink piggies, brown teddy bears, stars, or apples (add details with a black permanent marker).

You will need:

- ❑ Tracing paper and pen
- ❑ Scissors
- ❑ Stiff cardboard or plastic lid (from dairy container)
- ❑ Red felt, 8" x 10" (20 cm x 25 cm)
- ❑ Tacky glue
- ❑ Red yarn and masking tape (or cord or ribbon)
- ❑ Two medium jingle bells or liberty bells

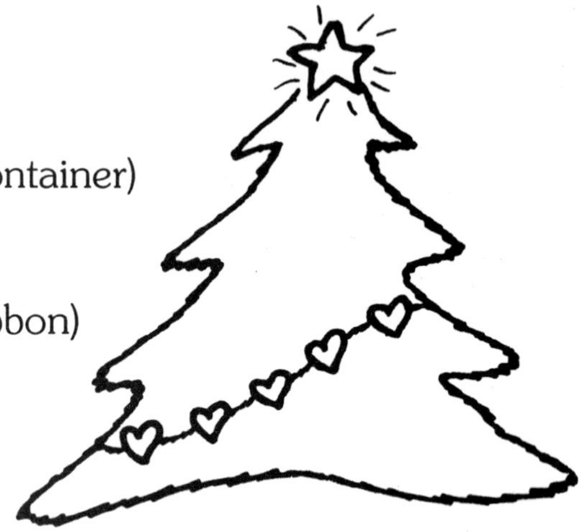

What to do:

1. Trace the pattern onto tracing paper and cut it out. Then trace the heart onto stiff cardboard or plastic lid (to make a sturdy pattern) and cut it out. Use the sturdy pattern to trace ten hearts onto the red felt and cut them out.

2. Take a piece of red yarn, about 2 1/2 yards long (2.3 metres). Tape one end securely to something solid (like a refrigerator). Hold the loose end firmly and twist it to one side over and over until it is tightly twisted. Then fold the yarn in half and it will twist around itself into a nice cord. Remove the masking tape. (Instead of yarn, you may use a piece of cord or ribbon.) Tie a jingle bell to each end.

3. Your cord should be about a yard long (90 cm). Start in the middle of the cord. With tacky glue, glue two hearts back-to-back with the cord in the middle. Then glue the remaining hearts back-to-back on each side, spaced 5" (13 cm) apart, as shown in the illustration. Hang the row on the tree.

4. Hearts can also be made from different colors or even foil paper. You can also make a longer string with dozens of hearts!

SANTA'S ELVES CARD AND BOOKMARK

Construction paper and felt scraps make marvellous Christmas cards. Use a toothpick to dab a tiny bit of glue behind the eye and mouth pieces to glue them in place. Anyone can buy a card, but a homemade card is always unique.

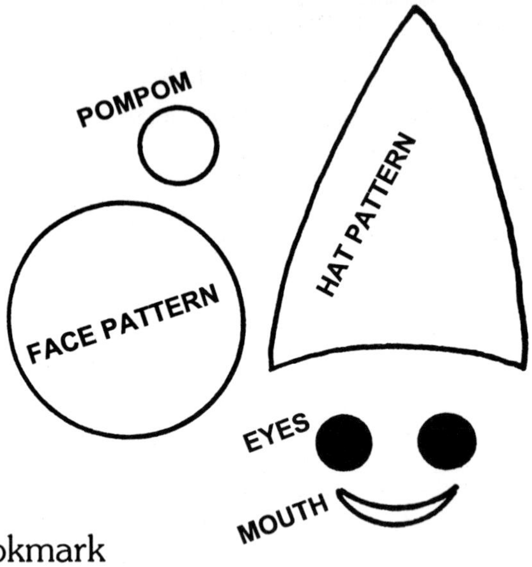

You will need:

- ❑ Green construction paper
- ❑ Tracing paper, ruler and pencil
- ❑ Scissors
- ❑ Red, white and black felt scraps
- ❑ Red, white and black construction paper
- ❑ Tacky glue
- ❑ Glue stick
- ❑ Black marker

Optional:

- ❑ Hole puncher and red ribbon for the bookmark

CARD:
What to do:

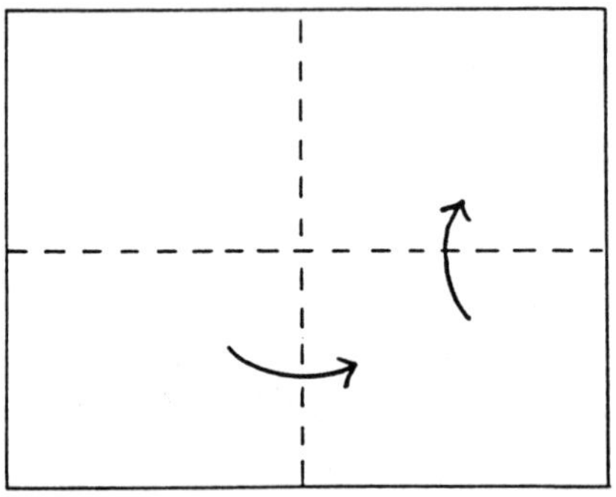

1. Fold a sheet of construction paper in half. Then fold it in half again, as shown. The folded card now has four layers.

2. Trace the patterns onto tracing paper and cut them out. Cut the faces and pompoms from white felt, the mouths and hats from red felt, and the eyes from black felt. Using tacky glue, first glue on the faces, then the hats, then the pompoms, eyes and mouths.

3. Write a message on front and inside the card.

BOOKMARK:
What to do:

1. Cut a rectangular bookmark from green construction paper.

2. Trace the patterns and cut the parts, as for the card, but from the construction paper instead of felt. Glue the elves on the bookmark with a glue stick.

3. Write a message on the front and back.

4. If you want to add a ribbon, punch a hole at the top. Fold the ribbon in half, push the loose ends through the hole from front to back (leaving the loop on the front side), and then push the loose ends through the center loop (twice, if necessary) and pull tight.

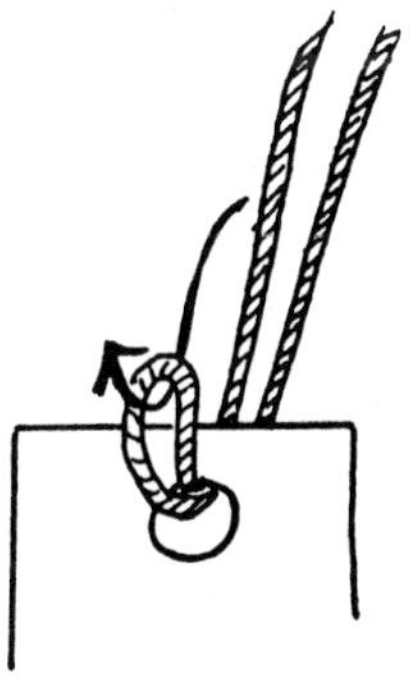

CRANBERRY RING

Anyone can make this simple wreath in a few minutes. The small beads won't fall off the chenille stem so it is easy for little fingers to handle. It makes a charming Christmas ornament.

You will need:

- ❑ 20 red wooden beads, 1/4” (6 mm)
- ❑ Red chenille stem or tinsel stem (metallic pipe cleaner), 12" (30 cm)
- ❑ 12” (30 cm) of fancy string

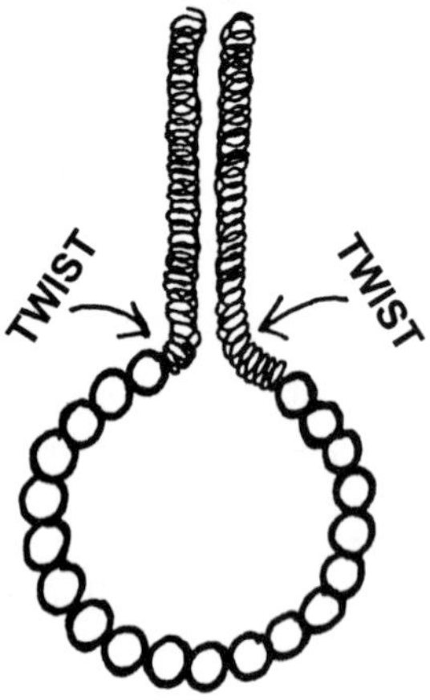

What to do:

1. Push the chenille stem through the beads. Form a circle with the beads in the center and an even length of chenille stem on each side.

2. Twist the chenille stem ends together at the top of the wreath, then spread them apart, toward each side.

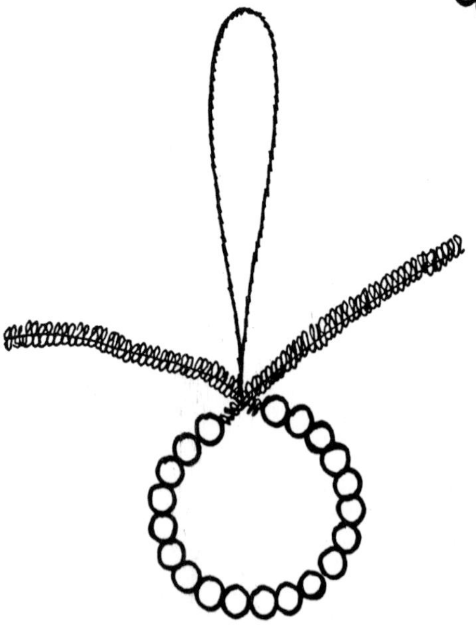

3. Tie string into a loop around the top.

4. Fold each loose end of the chenille stem toward the center and twist them around into a bow.

GIFT LIST

Name	Gift	Page

INDEX

Leila Peltosaari Albala at the age of 10. Leila grew up in rural Finland with her three sisters. Their parents were farmers. Now, with two children of her own, Leila lives in historic Chambly, near Montreal, Canada.

EASTER PIÑATA, page 60 EASTER BUNNY BASKET, page 58

FREDDIE THE SNOWMAN
page 92

LOVE ROW TREE ORNAMENT, page 96

SLEEPY ANGEL
page 82

GLITTERING ANGEL, page 78
SNOWFLAKE ANGELS, page 62

RAFFIA WREATH (75)
CHRISTMAS TREE BAUBLE (94)
CRANBERRY CLUSTER (66)

SANTA'S LITTLE HELPER
page 90